small
bites big
nights

Seductive Little Plates for
Intimate Occasions and Lavish Parties

small
bites big
nights

Govind Armstrong

with Ann Wycoff and Alison Clare Steingold

Photographs by Lisa Romerein
Foreword by Tyler Florence

Clarkson Potter / Publishers
New York

To my loving mother, Thelma,
and in loving memory of my father, William

Library of Congress Cataloging-in-Publication Data
    Armstrong, Govind.
    Small bites, big nights: seductive little plates for intimate occasions and lavish parties / Govind Armstrong
with Ann Wycoff and Alison Clare Steingold; photographs by Lisa Romerein; foreword by Tyler Florence.
Includes index.
1. Entertaining.   2. Cookery.   I. Wycoff, Ann.   II. Steingold, Alison Clare.   III. Title.
TX731.A74   2007
642'.4—dc22   2006015271

ISBN: 978-0-307-33793-1

Printed in China

Design by Maureen Erbe, Rita Sowins / Erbe Design

10 9 8 7 6 5 4 3 2 1

First Edition

acknowledgments

I have truly been looking forward to this stage of the writing process, when I get to give heartfelt thanks to everyone who has contributed in his or her own way to the creation of this book.

First of all, huge thanks to my family for their understanding, especially when I disappeared for months at a time while working on this project, and for being there when I really needed your assistance and participation. Thank you to John Arend, Indra, Chandra, Viruna, and your loved ones.

Lisa Romerein, thank you for capturing the simplicity and attention to detail we put into our food with your incredible photographs. I felt very privileged to work with you on each frame of the food shots taken at Table 8. You captured the essence of my food and my world—and your lifestyle shots are exceptional. Many thanks to your hard-working assistants as well. And, Eric, you were a brilliant wingman throughout the photo shoots.

I am indebted to Andrew Kirschner, my former business partner and chef de cuisine at Table 8 in Los Angeles. You are truly a great friend and we've shared memorable times in and out of the kitchen!

To the staff of Table 8 restaurant, who have made this restaurant so unique and wonderful. I applaud both the front of the house and the back, those who have moved on and those who have come through, and, especially, the people who have been with me from the beginning. There are the true lifers like Javier, who has been with me for at least ten years—*gracias, jefe*—and Frankie, Carlos, Manny: You guys are so intense! All of you make for a very strong team and have become part of the family.

Of course, there would be no Table 8 if it were not for our loyal customers who have supported us through the years. Many thanks as well to all the farmers and purveyors of the amazing ingredients we use at the restaurant.

To my partners at The Meridian Entertainment Group, Chris Heyman and Josh Woodward. I am grateful for your complete encouragement and support of my book. I would also like to thank our small group of investors for making Table 8 a reality and believing in me. To Reid Strathearn, my manager, you have done so much for me, from watching my back and keeping me organized, to making me more effective and pushing me to pursue projects with your aggressive guerrilla style. I love it! Thank you!

To Roger and Carmen Stuhlmueller, it was a great honor to shoot at your beautiful vineyard. And to Fritz, the ultimate host, thank you for your incredible generosity and passion for good wine and crazy times.

Thanks to Greg Peck, the partners of Peck Moss Hotel Group, and Fausto and Kathia Molina for use of your locations.

Thanks to my longtime friend Christian Caiazzo for his cheese knowledge.

To Lydia Wills, my stellar agent, thanks for protecting me and understanding my shortcomings in this new venture. To Jason Yarn, her assistant, props for your hard work.

To my editor, Aliza Fogelson, I am grateful for your patience, understanding, and direction. You stood by me and gave us great guidance all along the journey. Thanks for your enthusiasm and passion for this project. You are the best! I would also like to thank Marysarah Quinn, Camille Smith, Maria Gagliano, Joan Denman, and the rest of the Clarkson Potter team.

Ann Wycoff, your persistence was integral to this project. You were able to take my rambling and turn it into a book. After briefly discussing the concept of this book together, you totally got it. I am so glad I met you, and I would not have had anyone else on my side for this daunting project.

Alison Steingold, you and I definitely spent some quality time writing this book and testing recipes. Thank you for straightening out my sometimes winding train of thought and making it all possible.

And finally, thanks to my soulmate and love, Tina, for being so strong, solid, and my breath of fresh air throughout my roller-coaster ride. Talk about foundation! I could not have done this without you.

contents

foreword

I think Govind Armstrong is the culinary king of Los Angeles and I want to tell everybody about it.

The culinary world has been deeply rooted in his blood since childhood. Govind's resume reads like a Who's Who of the restaurant industry. From Wolfgang Puck and Nancy Silverton to Joachim Splichal and the "two hot tamales" Susan Feniger and Mary Sue Milliken, Govind has had the most brilliant opportunity to work with so many legendary members of the culinary world. Goat cheese, chanterelle mushrooms, nasturtiums, black cod, sea beans, heirloom tomatoes, green garlic . . . At the peak of the California food revolution, Govind was soaking it all up and identified with it completely.

After almost twenty years of honing his craft, Govind Armstrong is an amazing chef at the top of his game and only getting better. His restaurant, Table 8, in Los Angeles is one of the toughest reservations to get. This book is full of recipes that will inspire everyone. His relaxed style will make you feel good about entertaining and confident in putting it together—and his fresh and focused food will blow you away. *Small Bites, Big Nights* is everything you're looking for in a cookbook. From great cocktails to small plates and brilliant desserts, this book gets to the point.

On a personal note, I am thrilled to be writing the foreword for Govind's first cookbook. He and I are great friends, and we've found ourselves in many a place cooking together. Whether we're hanging out in South Beach talking about his plans for the newest Table 8 Miami location, or trudging through the snow with coolers of steaks at the Sundance Film Festival, or sitting on the roof deck at my New York apartment having dinner, Govind has an instant rapport with anyone he meets and you can't help but feel like you've known him for a long time. He also happens to be a very good sport about being harassed by all of our friends, who beg him for his Grilled Cheese and Pulled Short Ribs sandwiches at every occasion. Anyone in the know at Table 8 knows that Govind only serves the grilled cheese in the lounge area, not in the dining room. Mature, respectable friends at our dinner table have been known to leave the table momentarily to order a quick grilled cheese in the lounge. Trust me, they are addictive. So consider yourself lucky as the secret recipe for the infamous grilled cheese makes its long-overdue debut in this book. Be adventurous and make them at home!

In my opinion, Govind is the brightest young cooking talent that Los Angeles has seen since Wolfgang Puck, and he will be one of the great ones to watch along the years. He grew up in the city's best restaurants, and now it's his turn.

Govind, I love your book.

Dig in...

Tyler Florence
New York City

My earliest food-related memories are of my family's garden. I am digging my fingers into the dirt, searching for young carrots and eating them fresh from the ground. When we first moved to Encino, we lived in a funky, old ramshackle two-bedroom house once owned by F. Scott Fitzgerald, the outside covered with overgrown ivy, the interior walls decorated with vibrant murals of sunsets painted by the hippies who preceded us.

My mother loved to plant things, so the yard was filled haphazardly with greenery, herbs, bulging fruit trees, and vegetables. I remember plucking strawberries by the house's perimeter, biting into tart Gravenstein apples and sweet Santa Rosa plums straight from the tree. Ripened grapefruit fell to the lawn in the winter, and old vines of Concord grapes sat patiently on little terraces in the back. The backyard was a riot of fruit and color, the air redolent of the sugary aromatics of an endless summer. Each season, as a family, we would take turns planting seeds, then tending rows of radishes, corn, asparagus, tomatoes, baby carrots, Brussels sprouts, melons, and cabbage. My mother was by no means a professional gardener, but her passion trickled into the soil, making everything bloom.

Over time, our house and family grew in size, and two new baby sisters followed. At around age eleven, I made the connection between the garden and the kitchen: I could actually plan a meal from what I picked that day. The enormous difference in taste when you pulled vegetables fresh from the ground astounded me. We also had a lot of chickens running around out back in the coop, so that meant fresh eggs. Unlike the other kids at school, when we brought hard-boiled eggs for lunch, ours still had feathers and blood on the shell (much to the horror of our peers). I'll never forget taking the chickens, many of which were like pets to us, on a drive in the family wagon one summer day. They sat frightened in their cages as we drove and drove. Finally we dropped them off, then returned home silently with a few iced crates. No one wanted to talk about what was in them.

My mother didn't like to cook much, but we had family dinner every night, and she loved to entertain. Having come from a big family who lived on the Caribbean side of Costa Rica, my mother thrived on the energy and bustle of a full house and became famous for her parties. Painfully shy, I sought refuge in the warm clutch of the kitchen, where I would mix the drinks or prep the food. Even as a kid, I recognized the distinct buzz and great energy generated when people congregated in the kitchen. Good times were had, so I happily planted myself there. I began creating hors d'oeuvres for these parties, writing up grocery lists and shopping with my mother.

In 1981, at a surprise party for a friend of my mother's, a woman named Barbara Andrews wanted to meet the caterer. When my mother told her it was me, she burst into the kitchen laughing and couldn't believe it when she saw a scrawny thirteen-year-old boy wielding a giant knife, wearing a tall paper chef's hat and oversized apron, surrounded by a colossal mess. (Though my mother tried to teach me to clean up as you go, I didn't truly grasp and appreciate that concept until years later!) Barbara and I spent a long time talking that evening, and she told me about the new restaurant where she worked—and about a chef named Wolfgang Puck. At this point, the only Wolf I had ever heard of was Wolfman Jack, but something told me it was not the same person so I kept my mouth shut.

She asked me point-blank, "Why are you doing this?" I replied that I loved cooking and wanted to work at a restaurant and own a place some day. She immediately told Wolfgang about me. He couldn't believe it, especially that I was only thirteen. So he said, "Bring me the kid!"

Barbara called me shortly thereafter and took me to the just-opened Spago. I'll never forget walking through the back door; it was a total madhouse with people running around, giant carcasses of lamb on the butcher's block, mixers that were taller than I was, boxes bursting with produce stacked from floor to ceiling, people peeling, chopping, stirring, yelling, and laughing. My eyes bulged out of my head; I had never seen anything like it.

Barbara took me into the office and introduced me to Wolfgang. For the occasion, I had donned my church shoes and best threads. I brought him a book of recipes (half of which didn't even work), clippings, and funny pictures of things that I had cooked. I didn't really know who he was, but I knew he was The Man since everyone was running up to him and asking questions. I was completely intimidated, physically shaking, and my voice cracked when I tried to answer why I was "into" cooking. I blurted out that I loved everything about food, from shopping to peeling. He then made a joke about my supposed affinity for prepping carrots. Flipping through my book, he told me that he was impressed with my passion and offered me an apprenticeship if I was interested. I squeaked out, "Of course!" The next thing I knew, I was standing in the kitchen, still wearing my Sunday best, a carrot peeler in hand.

So, at thirteen years old, I was working at Spago.

I spent the rest of the day trying to stay out of people's way, totally out of my element. And while I was trembling inside, I also felt good, even comfortable in that wild energy. It was a very cool moment in my life. The stress, the buzz, and the chaos intrigued me. At the time, Mark Peel was chef de cuisine, and Nancy Silverton was the pastry chef. Luckily, she took me under her wing and filled in the blanks—who the big players were . . . what the heck I should do. That summer, I got a special permit from school so I could work five days a week. It was a complete trip to be in that sea of adults, to be working in the early 1980s at the hottest restaurant seemingly to ever open. The talent was insane—everybody was on his or her game. I tried to keep up but couldn't. Nancy would make fun of me for trying to be perfect; it would take me hours to get through a case of baby carrots as I meticulously peeled each one. Thankfully, she also pushed me along. It scared the crap out of me every time I had to sauté apples for her tarts and flame them with Calvados, but she definitely taught me the ropes.

The line cooks helped me identify produce I had never seen before. Trucks from SoCal's reclusive Chino Farms would deliver the most shockingly beautiful vegetables and fruits. I thought we had good stuff in our garden, but Spago's produce blew me away. I loved working with new products and learning how to make stocks and basic sauces.

The place was ridiculously busy every night; I couldn't believe that we'd prep all day long and then it'd all be gone by the following day. I learned about the flow of a kitchen from back to front; but most important, I knew after my first day there what I wanted to do with my life.

My most humiliating moment there was the time I tried to prepare the family meal for the staff—a true disaster. I had grand plans to prepare a cheese and jalapeño soufflé (remember, this was the '80s), but little did I know it was impossible to multiply it to the size I needed. I got in way too deep from the get-go. I struggled trying to make a roux in a huge roasting pan. When I put the egg whites in Nancy's mixer, I am sure to this day that she put sugar in it since she was the pastry chef and she was always adding sugar to egg whites for meringue. Despite knowing something was clearly wrong, I folded it, dumped it in the pan, mixed it a couple of times, and shoved it in the oven since time was running out. Then, I hid.

Luckily, one of the prep cooks saw me going down in flames, so he threw some chicken in the fryer. When Wolfgang came in and saw my uneven, slightly burnt soufflé, he asked me why I had put sugar in it. I threw my hands up.

Let's just say I never attempted staff meal again, but the experience thickened my skin. I realized that I had much to learn and that I had better start asking the right people a lot of questions instead of hanging out in the background with the produce. Luckily, I was surrounded by a receptive all-star team: Mark Peel (who would later open the renowned Campanile with then-wife Nancy) taught me about organization and efficiency; Kazuto Matsusaka (now of Beacon fame) showed me basic knife skills; author Mary Bergen and Lissa Doumani (who now owns Terra in St. Helena with husband/chef Hiro Sone), in addition to Nancy Silverton, expanded my pastry knowledge; and Ed Ledeaux (the present-day pizza king) showed me the secrets of the wood-burning oven. In the end, Wolf and company let me stay, and I worked there each summer for three years, until I was seventeen.

Two decades later—following a culinary odyssey that involved manning the authentic tandoori oven and working every station at Susan Feniger and Mary Sue Milliken's City Restaurant; cooking at Wolfgang's Postrio in San Francisco and exploring the birthplace of California cuisine; reuniting with Mark Peel and Nancy Silverton at their incredible L.A. restaurant Campanile and canvassing Europe on many missions to find the best food and wine; serving as executive chef at Jackson's in Beverly Hills; working for Joachim Splichal at his esteemed Pinot Hollywood; and building Chadwick from the ground up with Ben Ford—I finally opened Table 8, a lounge and fine dining restaurant on Melrose Avenue in Hollywood. All of these experiences where I experimented with the freshest products, sought out unique flavors, and thrived in the high energy of the various kitchens and chefs, led to the creation of this book. Table 8's market-driven, seasonal lounge menu is the basis for *Small Bites, Big Nights.*

After years of working with different ethnic foods and farm-fresh ingredients, I discovered that small plates were the best way to tie together all of the knowledge I had accumulated. Lounge menus allow for freedom in creation. When you are making three or four dishes as opposed to one larger one, the diversity of flavors is more interesting as a cook (and as a guest). I much prefer a mélange of textures, tastes, and products when dining rather than being limited to one main plate. While traditional three-course meals have their place, the energy of small plates encourages people to share food and be more adventurous. They entice cautious palates to go beyond their culinary comfort zones. We see this happening every night at Table 8, a dream that has become a reality for me. In this book, each dish is a sensory experience and showcases my love for local goods, unusual spices and herbs, and surprising flavor combinations.

Small plates also make entertaining easier. I picked several dishes (serving, of course, a party of eight) that are not so labor-heavy (although there are a few more complicated recipes for seriously ambitious home chefs). Each chapter represents a different style of entertaining; the food and cocktails fit this framework—all straight from Table 8's lounge menu.

Entertaining should be loose. I try not to impose too much structure, as every party has its own personality. Many of the recipes can be prepped well ahead of time so you only have to focus on the last-minute presentation details as your guests arrive. You should be relaxed at your own party to set the tone. Ultimately, everyone should have a good time, so get your guests involved in the cooking process whenever you can. Also, if friends stop by unexpectedly, there are quick and easy appetizers and dishes in this book that feel and taste gourmet, but you won't have to spend the entire afternoon preparing them.

Remember, the party starts long before your guests arrive. I hope this book can add a little spice to your entertaining—whether you're cooking for a large group at a barbecue or for an intimate dinner for two. Enjoy!

Pura vida,
Govind Armstrong

pantry

Dress-Up
Aïoli: Basic, Green Garlic
Pesto: Arugula, Celery Leaf
Salsa Verde
Harissa
Tapenade

Marin8
Cracked Green Olives
Marinated Roasted Peppers
Pickled Red Onions
Quick Preserved Lemon Zest
Roasted Tomatoes
Brine Mix
Chorizo

Daily Bread
Toasted Bread Crumbs
Panko Dustin' Mix
Pizzetta Dough

Orn8
Sachet / Bouquet Garni

For any home chef, a well-stocked pantry is the key to a successful cooking adventure. Especially when unexpected guests are banging at your door, you're prepared with a complete culinary arsenal. There are nights when our restaurant gets "in the weeds"; these backups can happen for a number of reasons, and we might be behind anywhere from five minutes to a full half hour. That's when we have to think fast and get our guests something to eat immediately. If there's anything that we can send out on the fly, it will usually be made from a few pantry items whipped together. What's hanging out in the fridge or on the shelf—if you stock well—can be transformed at a moment's notice into a delicious fast fix.

favorite

items to keep on hand

Beans
White beans, canned and dried
Black beans, canned and dried
Garbanzo beans, canned and dried

Jarred and Canned
Sun-dried tomatoes, not in oil
Capers
Olives
Gherkins
Anchovies
Albacore tuna

Tomato Products
Tomato sauce
Tomato paste
Crushed tomatoes
Tomato juice

Peppers
Roasted bell peppers, canned in juice
Piquíllo peppers, canned in juice

Staples
Potatoes
Onions
Garlic cloves
Shallots

Oils
Extra-virgin olive oil
Canola oil
Olive oil blend (preferably a
blend of extra-virgin olive oil
and canola oil)
Grapeseed oil
Hazelnut oil
Walnut oil
Truffle oil

Vinegars
Balsamic vinegar
Red wine vinegar
Aged sherry vinegar
Champagne vinegar
Rice vinegar

Condiments
Soy sauce
Dijon mustard
Whole-grain mustard

Herbs
Fresh thyme
Fresh parsley
Fresh basil
Fresh rosemary
Fresh oregano
Bay leaves

Spices
Crushed red chili
Chili de arbol
Black peppercorns
Fennel seed
Coriander seed
Mustard seed
Cumin seed
Cayenne pepper
Hungarian hot paprika
Saffron threads
Sea salt
Rock salt
Kosher salt

Nuts
Hazelnuts
Walnuts
Pecans

Dry Goods
All-purpose flour
Rice flour
Wondra flour
Panko bread crumbs

Miscellaneous
Pressed figs
Quince paste

dress-up

Home cooks on the run often grab a pesto from the Italian aisle of the grocery store, but it's not as difficult as you think to create your own freshly prepared sauces. You can really taste the difference in elegance between store-bought sauce and one made with vibrant herbs from the garden. Boost common fish, poultry, and raw vegetables; doctor up soup that needs a little kick with any of the recipes that follow. Learning the easy techniques to make a few key dress-up sauces, from simple salsa verde to piquant Moroccan harissa, can take you from the ordinary to the extraordinary (not to mention impress your friends).

Educ8: Elbow Grease

At the restaurant, we always use a mortar and pestle to pulverize herbs and spices. I urge you to make the jump and do it by hand rather than relying on a food processor or blender.

Like many young cooks, I first learned about emulsification after reading one of Julia Child's books. But, my first mayonnaise "experience" was at City Restaurant. When I asked chef de cuisine Dennis Kenniger about creating sauces with this method, he sent me off to prepare a ridiculously large batch. He handed me a whisk, a two-ounce ladle, and a whole lot of eggs. Sitting there in the prep kitchen, adding oil in slowly while whisking away, I learned two things: Whisking is all in the wrists, and making five gallons of garlic-flavored mayonnaise will advance the onset of carpal tunnel syndrome.

This cold sauce can easily be done up with anything from a pinch of saffron for an exotic taste to fresh Parmesan for a super-rich, creamy accompaniment to marinated tomatoes and a fresh fillet of yellowtail. You can also adjust the strength of the aïoli by using less olive oil and more "neutral" oil if you desire subtler flavor. True flavors come out once the aïoli sits for a few minutes before serving. Best of all, this recipe will keep in the fridge for a week in a tightly sealed container. But please make sure that you use the freshest possible organic eggs.

Basic Aïoli

| MAKES: 2 cups |
| DIFFICULTY: Easy |

Garlic	2 small cloves, smashed
Salt and pepper to taste	
Yolks of 2 eggs, room temperature or cold	
Juice of 1 lemon	
Olive oil	1 cup
Grapeseed oil (or a blend)	1 cup

ALTERN8: Parmesan: Fold in ½ cup finely grated Parmesan.

Olive: Add ⅛ cup Tapenade (page 31).

Toasted Hazelnut: Swap out the olive oil for toasted hazelnut oil and add 1 teaspoon Dijon mustard after making the paste.

Saffron: Add a small pinch of saffron threads when you add the eggs.

In a large mortar, add the garlic and a pinch of salt and pepper; pulverize and grind. The coarseness of the salt will break down the garlic. Then add the egg yolks and the lemon juice to the mortar. Work the ingredients into a paste. In a very slow, steady stream to emulsify the mayonnaise to "Miracle Whip" consistency, whisk or blend in the oils. If it becomes too thick, simply add a few drops of water.

Green garlic springs up twice a year: in early fall and early spring. This is a screaming green goddess dressing I like to make in the springtime, when the garlic bulbs, which are in the allium family, have barely begun to develop. Green garlic (also known as spring garlic) looks like green onion but is far sweeter and milder than its robust cousin. This supple stinking rose in an aïoli makes for a heady, perfumed swirl in a hearty potato soup or a bright complement to a leafy salad from the farmer's market.

Green Garlic Aïoli

MAKES: 1½ cups

DIFFICULTY: Medium

Green garlic	2 4-inch stalks, cut into ¼-inch pieces
Extra-virgin olive oil	3
Yolks of 2 eggs, room temperature	
Salt and cracked black pepper to taste	
Dijon mustard	1 teaspoon
Juice of ½ lemon	
Grapeseed oil (or a blend)	½ cup

In a small sauce pot, add the green garlic and ¼ cup of the olive oil and simmer over low heat for 30 minutes, or until very soft. Drain the garlic, reserve the oil, and allow both to cool. Add the yolks, garlic, and salt and pepper to the mortar or food processor, and grind it to a paste. Next, add the mustard and lemon juice, then mix thoroughly. Begin to add the oil, alternating between the reserved oil, the remaining olive oil, and the grapeseed oil as emulsifiers. You will not need all the oil; only blend enough to reach a "Miracle Whip" consistency. It will last up to a week in the refrigerator. Store in a clean jar.

Educ8: Toasting Pine Nuts

Simple to prepare, toasted pine nuts may not keep long, but they add flavor and a nice little crunch. In a sauté pan over medium heat, toast the pine nuts until they smell nice and appear just browned. (Be careful not to burn them.) If you do accidentally overcook the nuts, they will gain a bitter quality. If you taste even a hint of bitterness, toss what you've already prepared. You're not going to hide that flavor in all the arugula; cut your losses and start over.

Guests come to expect a familiar flavor when they see a bright green pesto on a dish, but here, the substitution of spicy, emerald rocket for basil is slightly unpredictable and totally garden fresh. While many a pesto is "chunked up" almost to purée consistency with a blizzard of grated Parmesan and a mountain of precious pine nuts, I prefer to keep this sauce on the thinner side but not runny. It's versatile enough for pastas, for dipping, and as an alternative to tomato sauce on a pizzetta with a well-ripened smother of Cowgirl Creamery Red Hawk cheese and baby artichokes (see page 243).

Arugula Pesto

MAKES: ½ cup

DIFFICULTY: Easy

Salt	
Garlic	1 medium clove, smashed
Pine nuts	2 tablespoons, toasted and cooled
Arugula	2 cups stemless leaves, coarsely chopped
Olive oil blend	¼ cup
Finely grated Parmesan cheese	2 tablespoons
Cracked black pepper to taste	

ALTERN8: Make a parsley pesto by substituting the same amount of flat-leaf parsley leaves for the arugula.

In a large mortar, add a pinch of salt and pulverize the garlic and pine nuts into a purée. Slowly begin adding the arugula and olive oil until the desired consistency is achieved. Stir in the Parmesan cheese, season with salt and pepper, and serve.

Always the bridesmaid but never the bride, celery is one of those poor, constantly overlooked vegetables. I'm not exactly sure why; there are so many different flavors in one head of celery, from the outer stalks and leaves to the tender heart. Although more often used in stocks and reductions, the hearts carry a sweet and complex flavor that can make a beautiful finishing sauce.

For this pesto, I use the delicate yellow leaves of the heart. They sport a less pronounced celery flavor than the darker, greener upper and outer leaves. The zing of lemon zest with smooth olive oil in this pesto cries for a fresh piece of fish. At Table 8, I serve this particular sauce with grilled sardines and roasted confit potatoes, garnished with hard-cooked egg. Developing that dish was a bit of a play on the tunafish sandwich without the mayo. A final sprinkle of Toasted Bread Crumbs (page 43) on top gets flavor sensations running on overdrive.

Celery Leaf Pesto

MAKES: About ½ cup

DIFFICULTY: Easy

Salt	
Garlic	2 small cloves, smashed
Pine nuts	2 tablespoons, toasted and cooled
Quick Preserved Lemon Zest (page 37)	1 tablespoon
Lemon juice	1 tablespoon
Yellow celery heart leaves	2 cups
Extra-virgin olive oil	½ cup
Cracked black pepper to taste	

In a mortar, add a pinch of salt and pulverize the garlic, pine nuts, lemon zest, and lemon juice into a smooth paste. Slowly begin adding the celery leaves and olive oil until the desired consistency is achieved. Season to taste. This pesto will last up to one week in the refrigerator.

Salsa Verde

MAKES: About ½ cup

DIFFICULTY: Easy

Garlic	1 medium clove, smashed
Anchovy fillets	2
Zest of 2 lemons	
Salt and cracked black pepper to taste	
Flat-leaf parsley	½ bunch, coarsely chopped
Mint	6 sprigs, stems removed
Chives	½ bunch
Basil leaves	10
Grapeseed oil (or a blend)	½ to ¾ cup

Using a mortar or blender, begin by grinding the garlic, anchovies, and lemon zest with the salt and pepper into a paste until smooth. Thoroughly mix all the herbs in a bowl, and begin to add them to the mortar or blender gradually as you continue to grind. Alternate adding the herbs with a stream of oil until all the herbs are incorporated and the sauce is emulsified.
It will last up to one week in the refrigerator.

Learning the ropes in my home kitchen,
I always experimented with pesto, using whatever herbs were available from Mom's garden. But for ultimate inspiration, it must have been in some kind of Chez Panisse–purist moment that I discovered the beauty of salsa verde. Think of it not as a chunky salsa you find in a jar in a Mexican restaurant; we're talking a subtle kick of anchovy and garlic in a shocking garden-green drizzler that makes the perfect garnish.

Most chefs have their version of salsa verde; this one just happens to be mine. I start by using quality anchovies, lemon zest, and freshly picked herbs. And then, it's all about really good olive oil (please use the best known to man if you can). To get really creative, you can swap out different zests and infuse the pesto with anything from tangerine to fennel frond. And for a deeper, heartier dish like brined Kurobuta pork loin (see page 155) or a rack of Colorado lamb with pasta (see page 129), there's no better zing of acidity to offset the rich, juicy meat.

If you're a fan of down-home hot sauce, or of Asian *sriracha* or *sambal*, then you'll flip for incendiary harissa, a staple of Moroccan and Tunisian pantries. There's no "standard" recipe for harissa other than a traditional combination of flavors including smoked or fresh chili, coriander, cumin, caraway, and garlic. Generally, the orange-rust–hued sauce is mixed with olive oil to make a paste, and it's sometimes then blended with tomato to make a smoother sauce. I've tweaked it by toning up and down on the spices and using the clean, smoky heat of a roasted serrano chili.

I serve this fiery pepper sauce at Table 8 with grilled vegetables and roasted fish. You can use it to flavor soups or braised meat dishes and tagines. Try stuffing a little of the paste in an olive as a quick serve for a last-minute guest. Make up a batch of this stuff, and you'll find endless uses for it—and believe me, a little goes a long way.

Harissa

MAKES: ¾ cup

DIFFICULTY: Easy

Serrano chilis	6
Chopped coriander	1 tablespoon
Lemon juice	1 tablespoon
Cumin powder	½ teaspoon
Garlic	2 medium cloves, smashed
Hot paprika	1 tablespoon
Cayenne pepper	½ teaspoon, plus additional to taste
Dried mint	½ teaspoon
Olive oil	¼ cup
Salt and pepper to taste	

ALTERN8: Dilute the harissa with water or tomato juice to make a spicy sauce to accompany couscous.

To prepare the chilis, simply pierce the peppers with a nonconducting utensil and hold over an open stove flame, or place on a grill or under a broiler until the skin turns black and blistery. Place them in a plastic bag, seal, and allow to sit for 5 to 10 minutes. Wearing gloves when handling the peppers, remove from the bag; the skin should peel off easily. Seed and reserve.

Add all ingredients but the olive oil and salt and pepper into a mortar or blender, and pound or blend into a smooth paste. Slowly emulsify by drizzling in the olive oil until it forms a stiffish paste. Season generously with salt and pepper, and add more cayenne pepper if you'd rather have a super-spicy harissa. Pour into an airtight jar, cover the harissa with a layer of olive oil, and place the cover on the jar. This sauce keeps for up to two weeks.

Tapenade is one of those condiments I keep close by while I'm in the kitchen. It's a perfect, happy little snack I double-dip crusty bread into while planning and prepping for an evening. There are so many versions of this traditional Provençal olive, caper, and anchovy paste; some call for additional anchovies, some for drained tuna—and some are perfumed with exotic elements like toasted orange rind.

Instead of butter at the table, I use a silky, creamy Ligurian olive and serve this rustic dipper with a warmed sourdough boule. Many fans of the fruit of the olive branch will swear by the deep earthiness of the kalamata or the delicate black niçoise. Though you may use whichever olive you fancy, Ligurian olives from the hillsides of San Remo have a mellow, buttery character; they're just fruity enough and not too "green." They remind me of a sun-drenched drive I took through Liguria on my way from the French to the Italian Riviera. I stopped off to sample what's probably the simplest cuisine ever—just fresh fish, fine oils, and endless bowls of those aromatic laurel-brined olives.

Tapenade

MAKES: 1¼ cups

DIFFICULTY: Easy

Ligurian olives	2 cups, stones removed, rinsed
Anchovy fillets	3, chopped medium
Capers	2 tablespoons, rinsed and chopped
Garlic	2 medium cloves, minced
Marinated Roasted Peppers (page 34)	2 tablespoons, diced
Zest of 1 lemon, chopped fine	
Extra-virgin olive oil	½ to ¾ cup
Pepper to taste	

Chop the olives or pulse using a food processor until they are fine but still chunky. Place the chopped olives in a small bowl, and fold in the anchovies, capers, garlic, peppers, and lemon zest. Add the oil until your desired consistency is reached. I prefer a smoothness to the olive but an overall chunky texture with just enough oil to bind the spread. Season with pepper. Refrigerate in an airtight container for up to two weeks.

marin8

These are all simple condiments that can be prepared well ahead of time. When you need to get something onto the table quickly, they're ready to go. And like a fine wine, they get better over time.

One of the scarier moments in adult life: the first time a guest unexpectedly "drops in" when your pantry is absolutely empty, save for a few cobwebs and a lone can of lentil soup. (Note: All guests are hungry upon arrival even when they say they're not.)

In these situations, it's important to buy some time. If you make a big batch of these olives and seal them in a jar with a well-balanced olive oil that won't overpower the fruit, you can always pour them into a bowl, give your guests some bread, and keep them busy while you figure out what to feed them later.

A good marinated olive can be a lifesaver if you don't feel like fussing around with Escoffier-rich sauces. I originally served them drizzled over a delicate white-fleshed catch, a pike-perch sander. No sauce for the dish—just roasted tomatoes (see page 39), sweet caramelized escarole, and braised artichokes. The marinated olives are all you need as a finishing component.

Cracked Green Olives

MAKES: 1 cup

DIFFICULTY: Easy

Picholine olives	2 cups
Thyme	3 sprigs
Oregano	2 sprigs
Bay leaves	4
Zest of 1 lemon, removed with a vegetable peeler	
Cracked black pepper	½ teaspoon
Pinch of crushed red chili	
Extra-virgin olive oil, to cover	

Tap each olive with a wooden mallet or the back of a small sauté pan just hard enough to split and "crack" the olive to expose the stone. Remove all the stones and discard. Coarsely chop the olives and place into a medium bowl. Add leaves from the thyme and oregano sprigs, the bay leaves, lemon zest, pepper, and chili. Mix thoroughly. Place in a jar to display, cover with olive oil, and seal tightly. The olives will be ready immediately, but they will taste better with age and will keep indefinitely.

Marinated Roasted Peppers

MAKES: 4 cups

DIFFICULTY: Easy

Red bell or piquíllo peppers	5 pounds, or about 10 large
Thyme	2 sprigs
Aged balsamic vinegar	3 tablespoons
Extra-virgin olive oil, to cover	

To roast the peppers, place them in a broiler or on a grill to char the skins until blackened on all sides, about 15 minutes. Remove them to a plastic bag and seal it tight. Allow the peppers to steam and cool for around 15 minutes. (To reserve the natural juices, place a sieve over a medium bowl.) You should be able to easily remove the charred skins, though you may need to use a damp cloth to remove any stubborn black flecks. Do not rinse under water—you'll wash away the flavor! Remove the seeds and cut the peppers into 1-inch vertical strips, then place in the bowl. Pick the leaves off the thyme and add to the peppers. Toss together with the balsamic and place in a jar. Cover the peppers with the olive oil and gently tap the jar to release trapped air. Seal tight and refrigerate. They'll last for three to four weeks.

Marinated peppers are certainly a weapon in my pantry "arsenal." These smoky roasted beauties next to a bowl of cracked green olives will have your guests thinking that you're the next Martha Stewart. Grab some crumbly feta, tear up a couple of basil leaves, and drizzle on your finest extra-virgin olive oil—now there's a tasty treat! (And if you're really on top of your game, you can sprinkle some toasted bread crumbs on top for a crunchy awakening.)

Possibly the most versatile of condiments, pickled vegetables meddle their way into most every culinary tradition, from giant kosher dills at the deli and *ume* plums in Japan to German sauerkraut and French cornichons. Because they keep indefinitely, a good batch of pickled red onions will wake up Chinese leftovers or act as a companion to a luscious grilled cheese sandwich with pulled short ribs (see page 241). I first served this particular recipe to temper the richness of a refined duck pâté. Easy, cheap, fast: What better combination?

Pickled Red Onions

MAKES: 5 cups

DIFFICULTY: Easy

Coriander seed	2 tablespoons, toasted
Mustard seed	1 tablespoon, toasted
Medium red onions	3, julienned
Red wine vinegar	¼ cup
White balsamic vinegar	¼ cup
Sugar	⅛ cup
Bay leaves	3
Thyme	3 sprigs
Salt and cracked black pepper to taste	
Extra-virgin olive oil	1 tablespoon

ALTERN8: You can blanch baby vegetables (think cauliflower, carrots, celery, pearl onions, baby corn, and asparagus) in water to "sterilize," then put them into the same pickling juice as garnishes for cocktails.

Toast the coriander seed in a small, dry sauté pan over medium heat until its aroma is released, about 2 minutes. Add the mustard seed to the same pan and toast for 1 additional minute. Soak the onions in ice water, then drain and pat dry.

In a small sauce pot, slowly bring the vinegars, sugar, bay leaves, and thyme to a boil. Adjust the flavor with water if too acidic. Pour this mixture over the onions in a medium, heat-proof bowl; allow to sit for 5 minutes. Drain off the excess vinegar, season with salt and pepper, then toss lightly with the olive oil. Store the pickled onions in an airtight jar in the refrigerator until ready for use.

There's mad love you can make to a lemon. This quick preserved zest, a Mediterranean and Moroccan staple, is a way to transform a tart lemon into an edible condiment.

Though I have a separate method for making whole preserved lemons, this recipe speeds up what's normally a long process. Sometimes, we need the quick ones when we have a sudden hankering for the concentrated, salty-sweet flavor of sunny zests. Try using them in your Salsa Verde (page 29) or with a traditional braised lamb shank. Mince them up for a zingy vinaigrette. And, backing off the salt just a bit, the preserved citrus adds a mighty complement to desserts and pastries like a fresh lemon tart.

Quick Preserved Lemon Zest

MAKES: 2½ ounces	
DIFFICULTY: Easy	

Lemons	4, scrubbed
Kosher salt	¼ cup
Sugar	¼ cup
Bay leaves	4, coarsely chopped or crushed
Dried chili pod	1, split open and coarsely chopped
Extra-virgin olive oil, to cover	

ALTERN8: When in season, experiment with the Meyer lemon to get a vibrant and extra-fragrant dose of citrus punch.

Remove the zest from the lemons with a vegetable peeler (be careful not to take off too much of the white pith) and place in a small bowl. Toss with the salt, sugar, bay leaves, chili, and the juice of one of the lemons. Refrigerate for 2 hours. Remove the zest from the mixture, rinse, pat dry, and cover with extra-virgin olive oil to store in the refrigerator for up to a month.

Educ8: Blanching Tomatoes

Place tomatoes in a wire basket, then dip into boiling water. Keep them fully submerged for ten seconds, then set in a prepared ice bath to stop the cooking process. Allow to cool completely and remove immediately.

Making your own roasted tomatoes is definitely time-consuming, but it's about as labor-*un*intensive as you can get. Remember to pull them out of the oven; otherwise, you'll have oven-dried tomatoes that are just as tasty. Because they are the ideal garnish, you'll see these tomatoes in a bevy of recipes from a tender green bean and prosciutto roll appetizer (see page 121) to grilled pizzetta (see page 243).

Roasted Tomatoes

MAKES: 24 tomato "petals"

DIFFICULTY: Easy

Roma tomatoes	6, blanched and shocked for 30 seconds
Extra-virgin olive oil	2 tablespoons
Thyme	5 sprigs
Basil	4 sprigs
Bay leaves	4
Salt and cracked black pepper to taste	

ALTERN8: Experiment with different tomato varietals according to growing season. In the late fall, just at the end of the season when the bounty is overflowing, we take the giant heirlooms and get them good and melted. As a snack, the smaller juliettes work extremely well to pop into your mouth like candy.

Preheat the oven to 300°F.

Cut the bottom end of each tomato off so it will stand upright. With a paring knife, start at the top of the tomato and cut downward to remove the flesh from the seeded core (you can reserve the core for other purposes). The tomatoes should be in petal-shaped fillets. In a bowl, toss the tomatoes with the olive oil and herbs. Season with salt and pepper, then transfer to a nonstick cookie sheet. Slowly roast the tomatoes until they become a bit caramelized and the flavor is concentrated, about 45 minutes. You can serve these hot or cold, and they'll last for a week in the refrigerator.

Do yourself a favor and unlock the juicy potential of your meat, fish, and poultry by brining. This extra step—immersing a protein in salted water mixed with herbs and spices—not only enhances flavor but also allows the product to cook almost ten percent faster. Brined meat has less of a tendency to dry out, so if you accidentally, say, take a phone call and forget about the chicken roasting in the oven, it will probably still turn out moist.

Best suited for lighter meats like poultry or pork loin, this recipe makes plenty to keep on hand in the pantry. Just add water and you're good to go. For something like weeknight chicken breasts or grilled chicken thighs (see page 95), about two to three hours is all you need, while a sumptuous Kurobuta loin (see page 155) will command an overnight soak. In preparation of smoking a whole side of sturgeon, you can leave it a few days since the flavor profile of the fish will continue to change once it's smoked. And for that twenty-pound Thanksgiving turkey, you'd want to double the water to five quarts and use two cups brine mix for a long twelve- to twenty-four-hour slumber before the main event.

Brine Mix

MAKES: 6½ cups dry mix

DIFFICULTY: Easy

Whole juniper berries	2 tablespoons
Crushed red chili	½ cup
Crushed bay leaves	½ cup
Coriander seed	¼ cup
Fennel seed	¼ cup
Mustard seed	½ cup
Dried thyme	1 cup
Kosher salt	1½ cups
Sugar	2 cups

ALTERN8: Feel free to swap out your aromatics, depending on the product you're brining. For example, clove is a nice complement to pork and will work well with chicken in lighter doses. A natural match to lamb, dried rosemary packs an herbaceous punch.

In a small sauté pan, dry toast the spices separately. Place all the toasted spices, thyme, salt, and sugar in a large bowl. Mix thoroughly. Store the mixture in your pantry in an airtight container. To make the wet brine, bring 2½ quarts of cold water to a boil, add 1 cup of the mixture, and stir until all the salt and sugar have dissolved. This is enough for a large pork tenderloin or 8 chicken thighs and you'll have plenty of mix left over for later uses. Place the brine in an ice bath. Once it is completely chilled, add to the product you would like to brine and place in the refrigerator.

Think of chorizo, and you're probably imagining hard and dried cured links of sausage. Characteristically deep annatto-red and spicy. Bold, fatty, and delicious.

With all the basic ingredients and a slightly different method, this form of Spanish-Portuguese chorizo is not a link. Without the casing, you get a natural form of sausage that cooks easily. Best of all, you can really taste the caramelization of the meat itself.

Not quite as greasy or high in fat content as some of the chorizo you'll find on a charcuterie platter, this one's a soft crumble preparation that's equally traditional and far more useful for my purposes as a cook. You can flatten the loose sausage into your hand and wrap it around hard-boiled quail eggs and fry them (see page 235); enhance a holiday stuffing; sprinkle religiously into soups and stews . . . the possibilities are endless.

Twenty-four hours of prep are required for this recipe, but it's worth the effort. And taking the time to marinate the meat is recommended but not mandatory. When making a batch, you can freeze smaller portions in resealable bags to bring out and doctor up weeknight pasta. It will also keep fresh for a week in the fridge.

Chorizo

MAKES: 1 pound crumbled sausage

DIFFICULTY: Medium

MARINADE

Salt	½ tablespoon
Cracked black pepper	½ tablespoon
Yellow onion	¼, diced
Garlic	1½ medium cloves
Piment d'Espelette powder	1 teaspoon
Hot paprika	1½ tablespoons
Turmeric	½ teaspoon
Crushed red chili	½ tablespoon
Ground cumin	½ teaspoon
Ground coriander	¼ teaspoon
Water	1½ tablespoons
Sherry vinegar	1½ tablespoons
Diced pork shoulder	1 pound
Diced pork fat	2½ ounces

Place all ingredients for the marinade in a food processor and purée until smooth. Remove to a medium bowl. Add the pork shoulder and pork fat to the marinade and mix thoroughly. Place covered in the refrigerator for 24 hours if you have the time, and be sure to chill the grinder attachments hours before use. Then grind using a large die.

To use, brown to taste or store in an airtight container for later use.

daily bread

Taking the extra time to make your own bread crumbs, pizzetta dough, or panko mix results in an infinitely better end product. Each of these basic recipes is actually quite easy to prepare. Feel free to alter with your own spices, infusions, and herbs.

Everybody loves the house "crumb"—not to be confused with standard breading or bread crumbs pulsed super fine—which we toast specifically for garnish. I like to keep them on the chunkier side when we hand-chop them at the restaurant; you get a more pleasant crunch and better citrus undertones, and the saltiness from the bits of fried caper combines well with flecks of herbaceous parsley and thyme.

Our bread crumbs are made daily, but you can store the bread crumbs in an airtight container for up to a week—if you can keep from snacking on them! Toasted bread crumbs are a perfect sprinkler atop practically anything, from saffron risotto (see page 181) to a seared fillet of rare yellowtail (see page 151).

Toasted Bread Crumbs

MAKES: 2 cups

DIFFICULTY: Medium

Stale bread, levain or country-style	4 slices
Garlic	1 clove
Capers	1 tablespoon, rinsed
Thyme	2 sprigs
Flat-leaf parsley	6 sprigs, leaves removed
Grapeseed or canola oil, for frying	
Zest of ¼ lemon, finely grated and placed on paper towel to dry	

ALTERN8: Reserve the oil after frying the capers and herbs. You can mix it with chopped fresh capers, diced shallot, and a touch of lemon juice and zest for an amazing caper relish to serve with a piece of smoked fish or a rare roasted beef.

Preheat the oven to 300°F.

Remove the crust from the bread, place on a baking sheet, and bake for 10 minutes. Rub each slice of bread with the garlic clove a couple of times, and continue to bake until golden brown and thoroughly toasted. Flip once, halfway through the cooking time (which can be anywhere from 30 minutes to 1 hour, depending on the staleness of the bread).

Beginning with no heat in a medium frying pan, place the capers, thyme, and parsley in ¼ inch of grapeseed oil. Heat to medium-high, and fry until crisp. The thyme and parsley will fry faster, so remove them first. When done, the capers will "blossom" and no bubbles will appear in the oil. Be careful not to burn the herbs. Remove the fried herbs to paper towels to drain; this will dry the herbs quickly. Let cool; chop coarse.

On a clean work surface, smash the slices of bread with the flat blade of a knife (like with garlic), then coarsely hand-chop the bread crumbs to tiny chunks and transfer to a small bowl. Toss with the fried herbs and capers and the lemon zest. Store in an airtight container for up to two weeks.

A good fry mix can make the difference between frumpy fried chicken and extra-tasty-crispy! An airy and light sweet Japanese bread crumb, panko traditionally lends itself to seafood but works especially well with cutlets and fritters and can be found at Amazon.com or any Japanese market. Its ethereal texture keeps that delicate crunch when frying up nuggets of goat cheese (see page 57), Brandade Fritters (page 231), or plump olives stuffed with spicy lamb sausage (see page 69).

You can add any sort of flavor enhancer to our fry mix base for complexity. Using it practically plain (as we have here), you'll find a nice coating to lightly dust a soft-shell crab. For something like a spicy deep-fried quail, you might toss in a pinch of finely ground coriander and fennel seed to add a bit more country flavor.

Panko Dustin' Mix

MAKES: 1½ cups

DIFFICULTY: Easy

Panko bread crumbs	2 cups
Cornstarch	¼ cup
Cayenne pepper	1 teaspoon
Chopped thyme	1 tablespoon

Finely grind the panko in a food processor. Mix all ingredients together, and store in an airtight container.

Educ8: Egg Wash

My basic egg wash—that all-important "binding" step in the assembly line of frying foods—takes 1 large egg to 1 tablespoon water. Beat together, and pop your floured fritters in there before a roll in the panko dustin' mix.

If you're able to keep the pantry stocked with this frozen pizzetta dough—definitely a trusty crust—then a quick nibble on the fly is always just a few minutes away. The Grilled Pizzetta recipe on page 243 offers some possible ways to prepare and top your pizza, but the options are limitless. Even when it's a late night and you're tempted to call the pizza man, remember that homemade tastes so much better!

Pizzetta Dough

MAKES: 18 2-ounce portions

DIFFICULTY: Medium

Sugar	⅛ cup
Warm filtered water	½ cup
Yeast	½ ounce dry or 1 ounce fresh
Bread flour	3 cups
Salt	5 teaspoons
Olive oil blend	½ cup
Whole milk	½ cup

Place the sugar, warm water, and yeast in a large bowl. Set in a warm place to activate the yeast, allowing it to feed for 15 minutes.

In a separate bowl, sift the flour and salt together, then add the oil, milk, and activated yeast blend. Knead the dough until all the ingredients are thoroughly incorporated. Cover the bowl with plastic wrap, set it in a warm spot in the kitchen, and let the dough double in size, about 30 minutes. Punch the dough down and repeat this two more times.

Divide the dough into 18 individual portions. Ball them up, brush lightly with olive oil, then wrap up tightly in a square of plastic wrap and freeze.

To use the dough, defrost slowly at room temperature, then remove from plastic.

orn8

The bouquet garni is a must for any cook, amateur or professional. A staple of the French kitchen since the seventeenth century (when palates became more refined and began to tire of so much heavily spiced medieval food, and when spices became more readily available), it's quickly made with fresh herbs and left to hang dry.

These little packages of herbs (either tied between leek tops or in cheesecloth) can be plopped into soups and stocks, legumes and beans for an extra hit of flavor. The sachet is used when the finished sauce will not be strained, while the bouquet is used when the stock will be strained. Of course, the French thought to endow a refreshing bundle of parsley, thyme, and bay leaf with its own poetic name, the *bouquet garni.*

Use a fresh bouquet garni at the beginning of each reduction.

Sachet / Bouquet Garni

MAKES: 1 bouquet or sachet

DIFFICULTY: Easy

Flat-leaf parsley	4 sprigs
Thyme	6 sprigs
Bay leaves	2
Peppercorns	1 teaspoon
Leek	1 dark green top, cut into a 5-inch length, washed

ALTERN8: Feel free to alter this mix to give a personalized tie-in to your dish; you can use the bouquet (or sachet) to introduce certain ingredient elements at the first stages of cooking.

For the sachet, wrap the parsley, thyme, bay leaves, and peppercorns in a small amount of cheesecloth and tie with butcher's twine.

For the bouquet, lay out the leek green. Place the herbs first, then the peppercorns, and fold it in half, securing the herbs inside. Tightly tie the end with butcher's twine.

celebr8

cocktails & hors d'oeuvres

Arugula / Dates / Parmesan

Tropical Summer Rolls / Sambal

Crisp Goat Cheese / Lavender Honey / Pumpkin Seed Oil

Burrata / Japanese Tomatoes / Panzanella / Wild Arugula

Duck Liver Toast / Fried Sage

Rare Tuna Crostini / White Bean Purée / Tapenade

Sea Scallop Carpaccio / Avocado / Cucumber

Seared Kobe Beef on Mini Yorkshire Pudding / Horseradish Cream

Fried Olives Stuffed with Spicy Lamb Sausage

Raspberry Slinger

Table 8 Sangría

Solid 8 Count

Table 8 Spritzer

Black Martini

I love having friends over to my house.

I wish I could do it more often. But when I do, it's a memorable event. Over the years, I have learned that it's a matter of having the right game plan from the start. Don't be overly ambitious; enjoy your own party! From pre-prepared and ready-to-go dishes to bites that the guests assemble to their liking, I always have a range of foods on my menu. Diversity adds to the festivities, so be sure to work with different flavors (from bold to simple and clean) and textures (from soft, gooey, and cheesy to crispy, fried, and juicy). Any party with trays of hors d'oeuvres calls for creative signature cocktails. Instead of offering an entire open bar (and finding a volunteer to man it), have a few specialty drinks up your sleeve that guests themselves can pour freely.

Educ8: The Garlic Love Rub

One of the most classic accompaniments to hors d'oeuvres (or a comforting bowl of just about anything) is a piece of toasted or grilled bread. At Table 8, after we brush a sliced boule or baguette with extra-virgin olive oil and cook it on a wood-burning grill, it's rubbed down with a raw clove of garlic. This imparts an upfront flavor of the stinking rose, then you taste a little bit of the oak. The bread itself has a nice glisten, and it acts as a bridge to tie together any dish that involves just a hint of garlic—hence, the "garlic love rub."

It has been trial and error for me to find the perfect bread. Generally, sourdough best suits my cooking style. With slight tanginess, rusticity, and "crusticity," and that airy pocketing with just enough spring to it, it makes for an ideal grilled or toasted bread.

Many of the dishes in this book take advantage of the garlic love rub. If you can, give your crostini or bruschetta that extra bit of love.

There is something about this classic combination that really speaks to me—and I love a salad that can be eaten with the fingers! Here, one of my favorite greens offers versatility. Its flavor will not only stand up to the "King of Cheese" and this ancient sweet fruit, but its simplicity is also wonderfully appealing.

Arugula / Dates / Parmesan

MAKES: 8 small plates

DIFFICULTY: Easy

Pitted Medjool dates	8 large
Diced shallot	1 teaspoon
Sherry vinegar	1 tablespoon
Extra-virgin olive oil	3 tablespoons
Salt and cracked black pepper to taste	
Arugula	1 bunch or about 4 ounces
Parmesan cheese	1 small wedge, for shaving
Sea salt	

ALTERN8: Stuff the dates with the Parmesan cheese, wrap with prosciutto or bacon, and sauté. Serve atop the arugula.

Stuff the dates with Chorizo (page 41), bake at 350°F for 10 to 15 minutes, then shave Parmesan cheese on top.

With your hands, tear the dates lengthwise into quarters and set aside. Whisk the shallot, vinegar, and olive oil together for the vinaigrette. Season with salt and pepper, then set aside.

Lay the arugula on plates, then sprinkle each with the torn dates, and top with shaved Parmesan cheese. When ready to serve, drizzle with the vinaigrette, then sprinkle with sea salt and an additional few turns of the pepper mill.

Educ8: Sambal

Of Indonesian origin, *sambal* can refer to a variety of spicy condiments or the searingly pungent sauce found at the Southeast Asian market. Move beyond Tabasco sauce and discover sambal; made with blinding hot chili crushed in a mortar and pestle, it packs a full-flavored punch. You can also find versions mixed with salt, citrus, vinegar, and even dried shrimp, but simple sambal "oolek" will work just fine.

A dipping sauce of sambal tempered with sweet, tangy marmalade and plenty of sliced scallions adds major interest to these mild raw vegetable snacks filled with crunchy-cool daikon root and anise-scented Thai basil. Sometimes they're deep-fried, sometimes steamed; I like to serve them raw because they travel so well. There's no cooking involved and these rolls require very little preparation. You can make them ahead of time and refrigerate until use; be certain, however, to place wet napkins on top of the rolls to keep them from drying out.

Tropical Summer Rolls / Sambal

SERVES: 8 as an appetizer or 16 for hors d'oeuvres

DIFFICULTY: Easy

SAMBAL DIPPING SAUCE

Soy sauce	¼ cup
Orange marmalade	5 tablespoons
Sambal	½ tablespoon
Rice vinegar	2 tablespoons
Scallion	1 tablespoon, thinly sliced in disks
Chopped cilantro	1 tablespoon

TROPICAL SUMMER ROLLS

Rice papers	1 package
Cilantro	8 sprigs, plus additional for garnish
Thai basil	8 sprigs, plus additional for garnish
Carrots	3, julienned
Daikon root	1 medium, julienned
Shiitake mushrooms	4, julienned
Snow peas	15, julienned
Daikon sprouts	1 package or 6 to 8 ounces

ALTERN8: To amp up these hors d'oeuvres, add cooked shrimp, chicken, seared tuna, grilled marinated skirt steak (see page 99), or any protein.

In a medium bowl, add the soy sauce, marmalade, sambal, and vinegar. Whisk together to dissolve the marmalade and thin with a few drops of water if needed. Add the scallion and cilantro; set aside.

Take all of the rice papers, and place separately in a bowl of tepid water for about 10 seconds, until they become soft. Pat the papers dry with a linen napkin, and transfer to a clean work surface. In the lower center of one paper, lay out a couple of cilantro and Thai basil leaves. Add a small amount of the julienned vegetables and the daikon sprouts. Pull the bottom of the rice paper over the vegetables, tuck under, and roll over one time. Fold over the 2 sides and roll again, as tight as possible without tearing the paper. Continue until all the vegetables are gone. You can cut the rolls or keep them whole. Garnish the plate with fresh sprigs of cilantro and Thai basil. Serve alongside the sambal dipping sauce.

Cheese plates are more popular than ever, and often, it's the accoutrements on them that win over the crowd. Guests learn to discover different flavor combinations, from tried-and-true quince paste with Manchego to decades-aged balsamic with a wedge of strong blue cheese. In this twist on cheese pairings, we use lavender honey and pumpkin seed oil, which is available at Middle Eastern markets, as garnish for delicate crisp nuggets of fried goat cheese. There's no need to purchase the finest chèvre at market; an inexpensive goat cheese log will do just fine. Best of all for doorbell guests, these can be made ahead, dusted with the panko mix, and frozen for up to one month. You can cook them straight out of the freezer, but make sure to brown them on both sides and finish by warming them in the oven.

Crisp Goat Cheese /
Lavender Honey / Pumpkin Seed Oil

SERVES: 8

DIFFICULTY: Medium

Goat cheese	1 8-ounce log, room temperature
Egg	1 large
All-purpose flour	½ cup
Panko Dustin' Mix (page 44)	2 cups
Grapeseed oil or olive oil blend	2 tablespoons
Lavender honey	4 tablespoons
Pumpkin seed oil	1 tablespoon
Toasted pumpkin seeds	2 tablespoons

Shape the goat cheese into pinball-size balls using your hands or a melon baller. Refrigerate for at least 20 minutes to allow the cheese balls to firm up a bit.

Beat the egg with 1 tablespoon water; set aside. In an assembly line, lightly dust all the cheese balls first in the flour. Remove the excess, then dip them in the egg wash. Finally, really pack on the panko mix. To keep the cheese from exploding in the oil and to make it extra crunchy on the outside, double-dip by rolling again in the egg wash and the panko mix.

In your left hand, place your index finger and thumb around each breaded ball and flatten it into a ¾-inch disk with the same fingers of your right hand.

Heat ¼ inch of grapeseed oil over medium heat in a medium saucepan. Sauté the cheese disks until crisp and golden, approximately 1 minute on each side. Drain the crisp cheese disks on a paper towel.

Arrange the cheese on a plate and drizzle with the lavender honey, pumpkin seed oil, and pumpkin seeds. Serve warm.

Burrata is a best-when-fresh cheese. It doesn't keep but for a few precious days. And why would we use standard run-of-the-mill mozzarella for this panzanella-caprese hybrid when one of the finest burratas from the family-owned Gioia Cheese Company in Pico Rivera, California (see page 252), is practically made in our backyard?

For those who aren't familiar with this seductive treat, the outer shell of the burrata is mozzarella. But once you cut or scoop into it, you'll find an oozy inside that is perfect for this dish. With a flavor that's slightly tangy and super creamy, the soft texture pairs well with the crunchiness of the olive oil–fried croutons. A sprinkling of wild arugula leaves sets the salad off with the faintest hint of spice.

My cooking is heavily ingredient-driven, so it's all about the best tomatoes (here, heirloom Japanese tomatoes), the freshest of herbs, and the best croutons prepared in a more-than-average way (fried until crisp in olive oil). The finishing touches make this dish, especially since the burrata allows other flavors to shine. We use "white" balsamic vinegar (which isn't actually aged in barrels the way name-protected Modena vinegar is) for a mellow flavor that doesn't impart the dark color of regular balsamic. This dish is a summer "ringer" every time it hits the lounge menu.

Burrata / Japanese Tomatoes /
Panzanella / Wild Arugula

SERVES: 8

DIFFICULTY: Easy

OLIVE-OIL-FRIED CROUTONS

Extra-virgin olive oil	1 cup plus 2 tablespoons, plus more for drizzling
Thyme	3 sprigs
Garlic	1 large clove, smashed
Rustic sourdough bread	3 slices torn into tiny pieces
Sea salt and cracked black pepper to taste	
White balsamic vinegar or red wine vinegar	2 tablespoons
Mini Japanese heirloom tomatoes	2 pints, blanched and shocked (see page 38), then peeled
Hothouse cucumber	¼, split lengthwise, seeded and very thinly sliced (on a mandoline if possible)
Red onion	½ small, thinly julienned
Flat-leaf parsley	3 sprigs, leaves only
Basil	1 sprig, leaves only
Japanese beefsteak/ heirloom tomatoes	4 medium-ripe, thinly sliced in rounds and kept together
Fresh burrata cheese	1 16-ounce tub
Wild or baby arugula	1 large bunch, about 6 ounces

Begin by preparing the olive-oil-fried croutons. Heat a heavy-bottomed sauté pan over medium-high heat. Add 1 cup of the olive oil, the thyme, and garlic. Once the oil has been seasoned for approximately 1 minute, remove the herbs. Add the torn bread, and gently fry while stirring occasionally until thoroughly golden brown and crisp, about 5 minutes. Using a slotted spoon, remove the bread from the pan, drain completely on paper towels to keep the croutons from becoming soggy, and season with salt and pepper. (You may reserve the oil for up to two weeks for similar uses.)

In a small bowl, whisk the vinegar with a small pinch of salt until dissolved, then whisk in the 2 tablespoons of olive oil and set aside.

Just before serving, to keep the bread salad from becoming soggy, place the peeled mini tomatoes in a small bowl, add the cucumber, red onion (to your liking), parsley leaves, basil, and the croutons. Dress the salad with approximately 3 tablespoons of the vinaigrette.

Fan a few of the sliced tomatoes just to the left of the center of each of 8 small plates. Drizzle the slices with some of the remaining vinaigrette, then place a small pile of the marinated mini tomatoes to the right of the slices. Spoon out the burrata right between the two, fluffing the plate with the arugula as garnish around the outside. Drizzle the burrata with extra-virgin olive oil, and season the plate with sea salt and a few turns of the pepper mill.

It's a miracle that I love pâté so much. Growing up, my mom would make calf's liver and onions about once a month—and she'd really kill the dish by cooking the life out of the liver. Everybody loved it, but I was terrified—I always felt like I was eating a brown crayon! Worst of all, I wasn't allowed to leave the dinner table until I ate my liver. Hours later, with my dog nowhere to be found, I'd still be sitting there with an ice-cold plate of meat. I'd take small bite after small bite, and finally, just as the eleven-o'clock news was beginning, I'd join the clean plate club.

Nowadays, you can't beat me off a piece of foie gras. Pure heaven: the quick sauté of the livers; a flaming of the brandy to burn off all the raw alcohol, leaving just the pure essence and flavor of a nice cognac.

The slight smokiness of bacon adds a layer of flavor in cookery that bridges well with grilled breads. Here, just a hint of diced bacon, along with nubs of butter, makes for a smooth and creamy final product that's beyond spreadable—it's like silk. Adding a sprinkling of Pickled Red Onions (page 35), a few crisp leaves of fried sage, and a garnish of sea salt on a crunchy toast will make you a believer.

Duck Liver Toast / Fried Sage

SERVES: 8

DIFFICULTY: Challenging

DUCK PÂTÉ

Diced bacon	2 tablespoons
Diced shallot	1 medium
Diced garlic	2 cloves, or ½ tablespoon
Thyme	2 sprigs
Bay leaf	1 large
Cleaned duck livers	1 pound
Brandy	¼ cup
Sherry vinegar	1 tablespoon
Sea salt and cracked pepper to taste	
Diced unsalted butter	½ pound (2 sticks), room temperature
Extra-virgin olive oil	2 tablespoons
Extra-virgin olive oil, for frying	
Small fresh sage leaves, for frying	
Sea salt and cracked black pepper to taste	
Sourdough bread	16 slices, toasted or grilled
Pickled Red Onions (page 35), for garnish	

ALTERN8: Instead of duck liver, you can substitute squab liver for a different flavor profile.

In a large sauté pan over low heat, slowly render the fat from the bacon; this should take approximately 3 minutes. Once the bacon is soft, remove it from the pan and reserve. Add the shallot, garlic, thyme sprigs, and bay leaf to the pan with the remaining fat. Cook until the shallot and garlic are translucent, about 2 minutes, making sure that the garlic does not burn. Remove the aromatics from the pan and reserve. Turn the heat to high, add the livers, and sauté for 2 minutes or less, stirring to keep them from burning, just until all the livers are seared but still rare. The liver should be lightly brown on the outside with a pink fleshy center.

Return all the other cooked components to the pan. Carefully and with confidence, add the brandy and flame, stirring constantly until all the alcohol has been burned off, then add the vinegar and reduce over medium heat for 30 seconds, or until evaporated. Season with salt and pepper, remove the thyme sprigs and bay leaf, and place the liver mixture on a plate to cool in the fridge.

Using a food processor and moving quickly, purée the liver mixture until smooth, stopping periodically to scrape down the sides of the bowl. When the livers are fairly smooth, add the butter in small amounts until all is incorporated and silky. Adjust the seasoning with salt and pepper and a few drops of sherry vinegar. Pass through a fine chinois or sieve. Spoon into eight 2-ounce ramekins, top off with the 2 tablespoons olive oil, and refrigerate.

Place the frying oil in a small pot. Add the sage leaves, and turn the heat to medium. Cook the leaves until crisp, about 1 minute. Remove them from the oil, season with salt and pepper, and allow them to drain thoroughly on a paper towel.

Serve the pâté with the sourdough toasts, some sea salt, cracked pepper, and pickled red onions.

Educ8: Stand and De-Liver

Begin with the freshest livers you can find. Give yourself the time to be specific and demanding of your butcher so he or she can order ahead. Even I need to order these livers about a week in advance so I don't get a flash-frozen waste of money!

When making pâtés, sausages, or any kind of forcemeat product, always use sterile equipment and surfaces. Keep any equipment that you'll be using (like food processors, spoons, tongs, mixing bowls) as chilled as possible. Place livers in a bowl resting on another bowl of ice while you're cleaning them.

Most important for livers, keep your ingredients nearby once you begin the cooking process. Duck livers cook up quickly. You don't want to overcook them (and you definitely don't want to undercook them). It's a very fine line, so do it right the first time!

On the aberrant evening when there's a mob of hungry diners in the lounge and a backup in the kitchen, I'll sometimes pull together these crostini as a way to thank my patient guests. Sushi-grade tuna, the best available, is consistently a crowd pleaser. Served seared and still rare on silky white beans, it provides two unexpected hits of flavor: one of spiced pepper from the spice mix; one from tangy olive tapenade. (Note: Please remember to soak the beans the night before to speed up the cooking process and result in more tender beans.) This dish brings together several components from our stocked pantry, such as the tapenade and the bouquet garni.

Rare Tuna Crostini /
White Bean Purée / Tapenade

SERVES: 8	
DIFFICULTY: Medium	

WHITE BEAN PURÉE

White beans	2 cups, soaked overnight, drained and rinsed
Onion	½
Carrot	½, peeled
Garlic	½ head
Smoked pork product (optional)	¼ pound bacon (or small smoked ham hock)
Bouquet Garni (page 47)	
Extra-virgin olive oil	¼ cup, plus additional to taste
Juice of 1 lemon	
Roasted garlic cloves (see page 120)	3
Salt and pepper to taste	

SPICE MIX

Coriander seed	¼ cup
Fennel seed	¼ cup
Mustard seed	⅛ cup
Black peppercorns	⅛ cup
Chili pepper	1
#1 sushi-grade tuna	10 ounces, cut into 1½ x 1-inch-thick loins
Salt to taste	
Grapeseed oil	2 tablespoons
6-inch sourdough baguette	1, sliced thick and toasted with the Garlic Love Rub (see page 52)
Tapenade (page 31)	½ cup

ALTERN8: Feel free to use the spice mix as a crust for fish, poultry, or even a slab of braised bacon (see page 155).

The white beans can be infused with fresh chopped herbs and oils and served with anything from pork loin to lamb and baby poussin. If you are in a bind, you can substitute canned, precooked white beans for the purée.

Try seared yellowtail for a different flavor. It's also less expensive.

In a large sauce pot, add the white beans, onion, carrot, garlic, pork product, if using, and bouquet garni. Cover with water, bring to a boil, then simmer for 35 minutes or until very tender. Once cooked, pull the vegetables and bouquet garni out. Drain the cooking liquid, reserving some for puréeing. While still hot, purée the beans in a food processor, adding approximately ¼ cup cooking liquid, the ¼ cup of olive oil, and the lemon juice and roasted garlic cloves to taste. (Depending on the size of your processor, you may need to work in two batches.) Purée until smooth and the consistency of a slightly stiff peanut butter. Season with salt and pepper and additional oil if it appears too chalky. Refrigerate while making the tuna.

For the spice mix, grind the coriander, fennel, mustard, peppercorns, and chili pepper together in a spice grinder or food processor, and pass through a chinois, fine mesh strainer, or sieve.

Place the spice mix on a dry plate. Season the tuna loins with salt, then roll the loins in the spices, evenly coating all sides. Heat a heavy-bottomed sauté pan (use cast-iron if you have one) over medium-high heat. (If your kitchen is outfitted with a window, now would be a good time to prop it open.) Add the oil, and begin to sear the tuna. If the pan begins to smoke, turn the heat down a bit and try not to inhale the fumes. Sear the tuna for 20 seconds on each of the four sides, then remove to a plate and set in the fridge to cool. Once the tuna is cooled, slice thin and set aside.

Smear the toast with the white bean purée, and place the tuna on the purée. Dollop with the tapenade and serve.

Sometimes a good scallop is hard to find. We purchase the freshest hand-harvested "diver" scallops we can source from Nantucket or Maine. There's a market out there that produces chemically treated specimens that should be avoided like the plague. Middlemen purchase smaller scallops from a source, then treat them with preservative liquids that enhance their appearance and swell them to a false plump. Since price and weight are mutually dependent, a plumped scallop will fetch more at market, so steer clear of the "soakers"!

In a dish like this, where the scallop is served raw, you need to ensure that you're using the finest product available—hence our use of sushi grade.

There's a clean, dry heat to a serrano chili that trumps the jalapeño's greener flavor. Here, it's all about pure intensity to play off the sweet scallop, the mellow avocado mash, and the cooling splash of cucumber.

Sea Scallop Carpaccio /
Avocado / Cucumber

SERVES: 8

DIFFICULTY: Easy

Avocados	2 ripe, but not overripe
Limes	2
Seeded and minced serrano chili	1
Sea salt and cracked black pepper to taste	
Hothouse cucumber	1, diced into ⅛-inch cubes
Finely diced shallots	2
Cilantro leaves	1 bunch, finely chopped
Extra-virgin olive oil	1 tablespoon, plus additional for drizzling
Sushi-grade sea scallops	8 "U-10," cleaned

Chill 8 small plates in the fridge.

Split the avocados in half, remove and discard the pits, then scoop the flesh into a small bowl. Squeeze the juice of ½ lime over the avocados, and mash them with a slotted spoon or potato masher but keep the avocado rather chunky. Stir in the minced serrano, season with a small amount of salt and pepper, cover with plastic wrap directly on the avocado, and place in the fridge to cool.

In a small bowl, combine the cucumber, shallots, cilantro, the juice of ½ lime, and the olive oil. Toss lightly. Place in the fridge to cool.

Lay each scallop on its side, and using a very sharp, thin blade, slice the scallop as thin as you possibly can. On each chilled plate, arrange the slices of one scallop in a tight circle, slightly overlapping, one slice over the next.

Put a small dollop of avocado in the center of each of the scallops, drizzle the cucumber mix on top, and squeeze on a few drops of lime juice and olive oil. Sprinkle with sea salt, add a turn of the pepper mill, and serve immediately.

I am a proud, card-carrying VIP member of Lawry's The Prime Rib. I've broken up with a few girlfriends, celebrated fifteen birthdays, fought with the family, and made up with the family countless times at this venerable Los Angeles institution. There are carolers during the holidays and college football jocks during Bowl Week chowing down on all they can eat. Then there's a bevy of servers who have been there for decades (and my favorite, Martha Cabasa, who works the door and doesn't make me wait two hours for a table).

This was the first item I created when we opened Table 8, and it is still one of the most popular dishes on our lounge menu. It is my bite-size version of the Lawry's specialty, swapping out large slabs of prime rib with small slices of Kobe beef. And a mini Yorkshire pudding with the kick of horseradish gives it that traditional feel. In this recipe, I use canola oil instead of the fat drippings from the whole roasted prime rib.

Seared Kobe Beef
on Mini Yorkshire Pudding / Horseradish Cream

SERVES: 8

DIFFICULTY: Medium

MINI YORKSHIRE PUDDING

All-purpose flour	1½ cups
Salt	½ teaspoon
Whole milk	1½ cups
Eggs	3 large, beaten
Canola oil	4 tablespoons
Prepared horseradish	2 tablespoons
Heavy cream	½ cup, whipped to semi-stiff peaks
Salt and cracked black pepper to taste	
Grapeseed oil (or canola)	1 teaspoon
Kobe flatiron steak	10 ounces
Chives	½ bunch, chopped

Preheat the oven to 400°F.

To make the Yorkshire pudding, mix the flour and salt together in a medium bowl, then gradually add the milk, stirring until smooth. Add the eggs and incorporate thoroughly. Allow the mixture to rest for about 20 minutes in the refrigerator.

Pour a thin layer of the canola oil in the bottom of either a mini 2-inch muffin tin or a large cast-iron pan, and place in the oven until really, really hot. Pour in the pudding mixture about a fourth of the way (it will puff up) in the muffin cups or to cover the bottom of the pan, and bake in the hot oven for about 20 minutes, or until there's no uncooked batter and it's golden brown. If you use a cast-iron pan, pop out the Yorkshire pudding and cut with round cookie cutters once cooled.

Fold in the horseradish to the cream, and season to taste with salt and pepper.

Heat a sauté pan over high heat. Add the grapeseed oil.

Season the Kobe beef with salt and pepper, and sear the beef to medium-rare (125°F), or about 3 minutes on both sides. Allow the steak to rest on a cutting board for 10 minutes, then slice into bite-size pieces.

To assemble this tasty snack, lay out the Yorkshire pudding, one per plate. Place slices of the beef on top, add a dollop of the horseradish cream, and garnish with chopped chives.

Somewhere deep in your pantry, I know you have a jar of cocktail olives. I did a survey to see what kind of ingredients my friends stocked in their kitchens, and olives ranked high on the list. So pull out that jar, make some spicy lamb sausage (no casings and a cinch to prepare), stuff the olives, and fry them up. It's an ideal combination of salty-briny-spicy with a delicate crunch of frizzled panko. If there are any sausage leftovers, sauté them and toss with your favorite pasta.

In a bind, you could easily stuff a little prepared sausage in the olives and roll with it, but making your own lamb sausage imparts just the right spice. I've also used Chorizo (page 41) for that subtle Spanish twist and served it with the Table 8 Sangría (page 73).

Fried Olives

Stuffed with Spicy Lamb Sausage

SERVES: 8

DIFFICULTY: Medium

SPICY LAMB SAUSAGE

Unsalted butter	1 tablespoon, chilled
Onion	½, finely diced
Chopped garlic	¼ teaspoon
Sherry vinegar	⅛ cup
Salt	
Ground lamb	1 pound
Cayenne pepper	¼ teaspoon
Hot paprika	¼ teaspoon
Ground cumin	¼ teaspoon
Pinch of ground fennel seed	
Pepper to taste	
Canola oil, for frying	
Giant cocktail olives	16, pimentos removed
All-purpose flour	1 cup
Egg	1 large, beaten with 1 tablespoon water
Panko Dustin' Mix (page 44)	1 cup

In a saucepan over high heat, melt the butter. Add the onions and caramelize for about 6 minutes. Add the garlic and sauté until golden brown, making sure it doesn't burn. Deglaze with the sherry vinegar, stirring constantly and working very quickly. You want the vinegar to evaporate but you don't want the pan to be bone dry. Remove the mixture from the heat and allow to cool.

Fill a large bowl with ice, and sprinkle salt on the ice to keep the temperature cool. Place another bowl on top and add the ground lamb, the cooled onion mixture, the cayenne, paprika, cumin, and fennel. Add a pinch of salt and pepper, and mix well with a spoon.

Heat a small sauce pot with 2 inches of canola oil to 350°F.

Split the olives almost all the way lengthwise, and stuff with the spicy lamb sausage. Place the olives quickly in the refrigerator to allow them to set.

Place the flour, egg wash, and panko mix in three small bowls. Roll the olives in the flour, then dip in the egg wash, and finally give them a nice roll in the panko mix. Place the breaded olives in the hot oil and fry for about 4 minutes, or until crisp and golden. Drain well on paper towels and serve immediately.

the right Cheese to please

Larger specialty stores like Whole Foods Market will offer good-quality cheese from artisanal makers, and these days, if you think ahead, you can order by phone or online, directly from farms or through stores like Murray's in New York or collectives like California's best, Cowgirl Creamery (see Sources, page 252). Remember, the key to discovering a beautiful cheese is knowing its origin. It doesn't have to be a classic appellation or a fancy name like Berthaut Époisses to be a fantastic piece of cheese. However, a dedicated cheesemaker using good milk will make all the difference.

The "when in Rome" factor of market-driven cooking extends to the cheese plate. If you're in California, there are hundreds of small farmstead operations producing gorgeous artisan cheeses. California cheesemakers are not just keeping up with the Joneses of Europe; they're now major players. I'm a huge fan of the collective efforts of Cowgirl Creamery, which brings together small farmstead operations to distribute across the country as opposed to considering them competitors and forcing them to fend for themselves. In addition to creating some stunning award-winning cheeses like the washed-rind Red Hawk and the buttery-mellow Mt. Tam, they're friends with, know of, and care about the other people making California cheese! If you're feeling like a little Frenchy Crottin for your cheese course, instead, try a soft log of tangy young creaminess from Goat's Leap in Napa or Sonoma's Laura Chenel (credited as the originator of American chèvre). Or maybe for something completely decadent, a Camembert-style goat's-milk Camellia from Redwood Hill Farm.

You can also find plenty of interesting blues and sheep's-milk cheeses that will knock off your socks. There's the now-famous Point Reyes Blue in Northern California, and also up in Sonoma County, fresh cheeses like the sheep's-milk ricotta of Petaluma's Bellwether Farms are sweet and delicate. And in the Southland near Los Angeles and San Diego, Three Sisters are making a stunning Serena, while Winchester Farms' Gouda is not to be missed.

I'm quite fond of Wisconsin cheeses, especially since their origin is a story about the triumph of the little guy. In some ways, Wisconsin hurt the industry when Kraft and major companies came in and began to create a cheese monopoly. Ironically, the backlash from mass-produced cheese was a small but powerful group of unbelievable farmstead producers who are making some of the country's finest cow's-milk cheeses. Pleasant Ridge Reserve, a non-pasteurized Old World–style hard cow's-milk cheese from Uplands Cheese Company, is a staple on Table 8's cheese menu. You can also order a fine selection of original Wisconsin cheeses through the Carr Valley Cheese Company.

Farmstead all-stars from other parts of the country range from the Pacific Northwest, where Sally Jackson's chestnut-wrapped cow's-milk cheese steals the show, to New Jersey's cave-aged sheep's-milk cheese from Oldwick Tomme—a perennial favorite of mine. Got the blues? Try the crumbly but oh-so-strong Bayley Hazen Blue, a family operation straight out of Vermont. All can be ordered online and can be found in our source guide on page 252.

You could easily load up a cheese plate with a dozen super-tantalizing offerings, but think about your guests and how much food you are serving. If the focus of your party is toward wine pairing, then think about matching individual wines with individual cheeses. Do try, however, to mix up your milks. If you serve three cheeses, try a cow's, goat's, and sheep's milk. For four, perhaps add a blue. And then, if you're going to impress, think about hard versus soft, fresh versus aged, and domestic versus imported.

FROM STORE TO STORING

Approach cheese as you would sushi; you'd never want to purchase cheese from a place that's not busy. More than with meat or wine, cheese is 100 percent dependent on who's selling it. If buying a pre-cut, plastic-wrapped wedge, you'll want to be sure it has been wrapped recently, and that it's the best possible cheese on display (and not two weeks old). The surface area that touches the wrapper decreases the flavor of the cheese, so select a larger piece that's cut with balance from rind to end.

When bringing cheese home, begin by keeping it cool in the refrigerator. Keep it loosely wrapped; otherwise, you'll have either a dried out or suffocated specimen.

If you're entertaining later in the day, try to take out the cheese around noon, or at the absolute latest, three o'clock. Most people will tell you to take cheese out an hour before you serve it, but most households are not warm enough to really get the cheese to optimal temperature. And then there's the worry that a piece of cheese at room temperature will go "bad" if left out all day. Yes, cheese is a dairy product, but it was also invented as a way to preserve milk through salting, curding, and basketing. Believe me, three to five hours on the counter isn't going to hurt you or the cheese. If anything, the cheese will be better. As it warms, the fat globules that hold the milk curds together soften so that your teeth will go through the cheese more easily, with a more pleasant texture. The cheese's soul and flavor will open up and flow.

It's best to unwrap your cheese and store it on a plate under glass. If you don't have a glass dome, then something like an inverted bowl will work so that just the right amount of air circulates.

While raspberry liquor has some people on the fence, I promise this drink tastes nothing like cough syrup. And you get the delicious little bonus of raspberry sorbet in the glass. I've been spotted at Table 8's dining bar, stealing a few sips from one of my sisters' "slingers."

Raspberry Slinger

SERVES: 1	
DIFFICULTY: Easy	

Stoli Razbery	1 ounce
Stoli Vanil	1 ounce
Cranberry juice	1 ounce
Pineapple juice	1 ounce
Raspberry sorbet	2 tablespoons

Fill a chilled highball glass with crushed ice. Fill a cocktail shaker with ice, and pour in the vodkas, cranberry juice, and pineapple juice. Stir thoroughly. Add the dollop of raspberry sorbet onto the ice in the highball glass, and pour the drink on top. Serve immediately with a tall straw.

Easily made for large groups, a semi-traditional Spanish sangría actually tastes best when prepared days in advance. I like a drizzle of honey and rum instead of the more traditional use of cognac or brandy. This is an easily altered recipe, so loads of fresh "drunken" fruit can be added; use whatever you have on hand to enhance the drink's potent sweet-tart flavor.

Table 8 Sangría

SERVES: 8 to 10

DIFFICULTY: Easy

Honey	2 tablespoons
Red wine	1 750-ml bottle
White wine	½ bottle (375 ml)
Rum	1 cup
Orange juice	½ cup
Large orange	1, thinly sliced, seeded
Lime	1, thinly sliced, seeded
Lemon	1, thinly sliced, seeded
Club soda	2 cups, chilled

Stir the honey into the red and white wines in a large pitcher. Add the rum, orange juice, and sliced fruit. Refrigerate covered for several hours and up to a few days. Before serving, add the club soda and pour over ice into wineglasses.

There is such a thing as a shot for "grown-ups," and this just may be it. Sweet but not cloying, with a vodka base, it's definitely a quaffable shooter. This was created on a late night with (coincidentally) eight of our closest friends in the lounge at Table 8. Andrew poured eight counts of vodka over ice into a cocktail shaker, and then added a bunch of other goodies. The rest, as they say, is history.

Solid 8 Count

SERVES: 8	
DIFFICULTY: Easy	

Vodka	4 ounces
Vanilla vodka	2 ounces
Vanilla simple syrup (see Educ8, opposite)	1 teaspoon
Cranberry juice	2 ounces
Fresh strawberry juice	2 ounces

Fill a shaker with ice and pour in the vodkas, simple syrup, and juices. Shake vigorously and strain into shot glasses.

Educ8: Infused Simple Syrups

Vanilla, passion fruit, and cardamom simple syrups sound gourmet, but they're all simple to make. They last forever, and they're especially eye-catching in glass bottles lined up in your kitchen or bar.

There's really nothing more to it than equal parts sugar to water. Use your imagination to choose various herbs and spices to infuse with, as we've done here with vanilla bean to accent the vanilla vodka and strawberry juice. Bring the mixture to a boil, remove from the heat, add your ingredients to steep, then allow it to cool before straining out the solids. Other recipes brewing:

• Lime-basil in a Basil Mint Mojito (page 104)
• Cardamom in the carroty Mirepoix (page 137)
• Sage in the pineapple-guava–kissed Sage Brush (page 105)

I often find that when entertaining at home, hosts forget to accommodate guests who either choose not to imbibe or are just pacing themselves. Rather than stick them with tap water or a soda from the fridge, treat them to a lively, puckery spritzer that's sure to please.

Table 8 Spritzer

SERVES: 8	
DIFFICULTY: Easy	

Fresh orange juice	1 cup
Cranberry juice	2 cups
Juice of 2 lemons	
Superfine sugar	1 cup
Club soda	1 quart, chilled
Slices of orange, for garnish	3
Slices of lemon, for garnish	3

In a large pitcher, mix the orange and cranberry juices with the lemon juice. Add the sugar and stir well until dissolved. Pour in the chilled club soda, and float the fruit slices on top for garnish. To serve, pour the punch over ice cube–filled highball glasses.

Table 8's longtime bartender, Sammy, worked with me way back when we opened Chadwick. (These days, he's over at L Scorpion as our resident tequila connoisseur.) Here's one of the most popular drinks in Sammy's arsenal. It may not actually be black, but it's certainly dark with deep currant flavor.

Black Martini

SERVES: 1	
DIFFICULTY: Easy	

Absolut Kurant	2 ounces
Cranberry juice	2 ounces
Blue curaçao	½ ounce

Fill a cocktail shaker with ice. Pour the vodka, cranberry juice, and blue curaçao over the ice. Shake vigorously, and strain into chilled martini glasses. Serve immediately.

from grill to pl8

Grilled Endive / Serrano Ham / Aged Sherry / Cabrales

Grilled Sardine Parcels / Braised Fennel / Meyer Lemon / Olive

Grilled Squid / Green Garbanzos / Bruschetta

New Zealand Scampi / Heirloom Tomato / Summer Truffle Vinaigrette

Barbecued Quail / Grilled Corn Salsa

Grilled Chicken Thighs / Wood-Roasted Gazpacho / Avocado Salsa

Grilled Skirt Steak in Lettuce Leaves / Soy-Ginger Dipping Sauce

Mascarpone Peanut Butter Brownies / Dark Chocolate Sauce / Honeyed Peanuts

Basil Mint Mojito

Sage Brush

Sparkling Summer Berry and Lemon Sangría

Watermellow

Sex on South Beach

Listen up, people: The grill is not only for hamburgers, hot dogs, and steaks (although I certainly remember our little hibachi that we'd use at the beach or when camping to make those very things). I have always enjoyed working with a live fire in restaurants and using different woods like white oak and apple (or even mesquite, which imparts a completely different, smoky flavor to meats). In my experience, the grill stations were always the busiest and most hectic; I spent many a year on different grills. It's a tricky place to work as you're cooking meats to a specific temperature or "doneness" for the diner. When grilling fish, it is crucial to pay careful attention so you don't dry out the flesh.

At home, grilling takes on a new role, one that's very relaxing. It's the focal point of outdoor social gatherings and a good place to get creative. At Table 8, we grill anything from escarole to cauliflower. Even for novices, an easy and impressive item in this chapter is the grilled Belgian endive with Serrano ham. Most people don't realize that certain hearty greens hold up extremely well to the lightly charred flavor of the grill.

So after firing it up, cool things down with some sexy cocktails like our signature basil mint mojito, and you've got a party (in and) on your hands.

A closely guarded, name-protected blue cheese from pastoral Asturias, Spain, prized Cabrales is one of the most complex and piquant cheeses in the world. With its telltale blue-green veining, Cabrales is hand-crafted with a blend of cow's, sheep's, and goat's milk that varies by season and reaches its peak in the summertime. I love its slightly spicy machismo and crumbly texture. This rich, aggressive cheese will overpower most subtle flavors unless you pair it with something like a fine aged sherry vinegar—a classic Spanish combo. And then you get the extra crispy, salty rush from Serrano ham against the caramelization of grilled Belgian endive for a punch of bitter-salty-sweet.

These "lounge spears" are so simple to make in advance and pull out just in time to throw on a hot grill. Be sure to get the Serrano golden and crisp, but keep an eye on them; when the shaved slices get too dark, an unappealing hammy bitterness will result. If you don't have a grill, you can easily pan-sear them with a touch of olive oil.

Grilled Endive / Serrano Ham /
Aged Sherry / Cabrales

SERVES: 8

DIFFICULTY: Easy

Baby Belgian endives	4, quartered
Cabrales cheese	2 ounces
Serrano ham	8 slices, cut in half lengthwise
Extra-virgin olive oil	3 tablespoons, plus extra for brushing
Aged sherry vinegar	2 tablespoons
Diced shallot	1 teaspoon
Salt and cracked black pepper to taste	
Frisée	2 heads, cleaned
Flat-leaf parsley	4 sprigs, leaves only

Prepare a gas or charcoal grill.

For each endive quarter, lift half the leaves and stuff with the cheese, then wrap with a Serrano slice. Set them aside until you're ready to grill. Meanwhile, in a small bowl, whisk the olive oil into the vinegar. Add the shallots, and season with salt and pepper.

Brush the Serrano-wrapped endives with olive oil and place on the hot grill, stuffed side down first. Cook the endives until the ham becomes crisp and the endives are cooked through. The leaves should be slightly golden and wilted, the core easily pierced with a paring knife. Toss the frisée and parsley leaves with some of the vinaigrette and season with salt and pepper. Arrange 8 plates with 2 wrapped endives on each and garnish with the salad. If you prefer, you may wish to dress up each plate with more crumbled Cabrales.

Grilling sardines directly on the grates can be awfully challenging unless you're a resident grill master; these quick-cooking fish will stick easily. To avoid the headache of grilling sardines, try using a parcel as a vehicle to house the sardine and all your aromatic components. Because the parchment paper is only on the flame for a minute or so, there's no need to worry about anything burning. For a fish that cooks slowly, like salmon or halibut, I'd recommend the traditional preparation *en papillote* in the oven (see page 126). To make this recipe, you'll need eight 7-inch squares of parchment paper.

In an attempt to get the sardine back out into the world, I served them using this technique at an event for more than 2,000 guests. The parcel method came to mind when I realized that grilling that many fish and plating them à la minute would be an absolute nightmare. So prep these beautiful parcels a day in advance, and pull them out just in time for grilling.

Grilled Sardine Parcels /
Braised Fennel / Meyer Lemon / Olive

SERVES: 8

DIFFICULTY: Medium

Fennel	1 small head, diced medium
Sachet (page 47) with ½ teapsoon fennel seed and pinch of crushed red chili	
Extra-virgin olive oil	¼ cup
Meyer lemon	1
Salt and pepper to taste	
Diced shallot	2 tablespoons
Chopped fennel frond	1 teaspoon
Fresh sardines	8 medium, head, scales, and bones removed and gutted
Roasted Tomatoes (page 39)	8
Cracked Green Olives (page 33)	¼ cup

Combine the diced fennel head, sachet, and olive oil in a small sauce pot; bring to a simmer. Cook the fennel on low heat until very tender, about 25 minutes, and allow the fennel to cool in the seasoned oil. Once cool, strain the fennel and reserve the oil.

Prepare a gas or charcoal grill.

Cut off either end of the Meyer lemon so it will stand vertically; cut into quarters. Stand up one quarter at a time, and cut straight down with a knife to remove the entire core and half of the flesh, reserving both pieces. Repeat with all the wedges. Cut the lemon zest and flesh into a small dice and place into a small bowl. Squeeze the juice from the core over the diced lemon. Season with salt and pepper, and allow to marinate for 20 minutes. Add the diced shallot to the lemon, as well as the cooled oil from the braised fennel. Stir in the chopped fennel frond, and adjust the seasoning if needed.

Lay eight 7-inch squares of parchment paper on a dry surface, and brush the center of each

recipe continues...

Educ8: Sardine Phobia

My eyes opened to the glory of the sardine during my first trip to Italy. I'll never forget the freshness of just-caught sardines in a café deep in an alley off the Rialto Market in water-logged Venice. They were lightly grilled and served with white polenta and caramelized onions, drizzled with good olive oil, with a few leaves of arugula—and that was it.

Why were these fresh treasures so overlooked in the States? Even on restaurant menus, the sardine void in Los Angeles was painfully apparent. True, a rolled-up tin of sardines is quite unappealing (along with any other canned fish aside from tuna). A sardine that's less than optimal will be fishy, oily, and overpowering, but a perfectly fresh sardine, like a good anchovy, is unbelievable. From that point forward, I was on a mission to debunk the myth that sardines are "gross."

Those who believe in the sardine immediately order them and are enraptured; those who don't are, in my opinion, missing out!

recipe continued...

with braised fennel oil. Over each parchment, give a pepper mill a couple of turns. Place 1 sardine, skin side down, on the paper. Cut 1 tomato fillet in half lengthwise, and place the halves on top of the sardine. Spoon on some of the braised fennel head, and a few olives on top of that. Fold the parchment into a little parcel, and tie with butcher's twine.

Place the parchments on the preheated grill away from the hot spot, and cook each side for about 1 minute. Be careful not to let them burn.

To serve, cut open the parcels and drizzle on the lemon relish. Salt before serving.

Buttery isn't a word that most cooks would use to describe the chickpea. But try a green garbanzo bean, and your outlook on this simple legume will drastically change. Green garbanzos only appear sporadically in California, so it's a special treat when they arrive; some farmers use them to till their fields, but we ask them specifically to save some for us. When braised, they take on a creamy, rich texture that's totally ethereal. Garbanzo beans gain a starchier, woodier texture the first time they're cooked through. As with a twice-baked potato, the extra step of braising them in olive oil locks in a totally different flavor profile. This dual preparation, both quick-marinated and smeared, on a crusty baguette with the Garlic Love Rub (page 52), offers a sunny, garlicky Mediterranean bruschetta cradling tender grilled squid.

Always be certain to only lightly grill your squid to just cook them through. Otherwise, they will become rubbery and inedible.

Grilled Squid / Green Garbanzos
/ Bruschetta

SERVES: 8 as an appetizer or

16 for hors d'oeuvres

DIFFICULTY: Medium

Cleaned squid	8 ounces
Fresh oregano	3 sprigs, leaves only
Zest and juice of ½ lemon	
Small pinch of crushed red chili	
Extra-virgin olive oil	⅓ cup plus 4 tablespoons
Cooked green garbanzo beans	2 cups
Sachet (page 47)	
Salt and pepper to taste	
Diced tomato	¼ cup
Diced yellow bell pepper	¼ cup
Thyme	1 teaspoon, leaves only
Aged sherry vinegar	2 tablespoons
Loaf of sourdough bread	
Garlic	1 medium clove, peeled

ALTERN8: If you cannot source green garbanzos, look for dried green varieties or dried black. Or drain a canned version, then braise in good-quality extra-virgin olive oil.

Serve with a tangy aïoli (see pages 23 and 25).

Place the squid in a small bowl. Squeeze the oregano leaves to release the fragrant oils, and place on top of the squid. Add the lemon zest, crushed red chili, and 3 tablespoons of the olive oil, and allow the squid to marinate for at least 30 minutes.

While the squid is marinating, place the garbanzo beans in a small pot, and cover with the ⅓ cup of olive oil. Pop in the sachet as well. Simmer for at least 30 minutes, stirring often and allowing the beans to swell and become creamy and buttery (and delicious). Remove from the heat and allow the beans to cool in the oil. Drain once cooled, and reserve the oil for later use.

Prepare a gas or charcoal grill.

Place half the cooked beans in a bowl; add half the lemon juice and the remaining tablespoon of olive oil. Season with salt and pepper and, with a potato masher, mash the beans into a paste. Set aside.

Place the remaining beans with the tomato, bell pepper, thyme, vinegar, and remaining lemon juice in a medium bowl. Season with salt and pepper, and allow this mixture to marinate for 15 minutes.

Cut the bread loaf on a bias in ½-inch-thick slices and give it the Garlic Love Rub (page 52).

Season the marinated squid with salt and pepper, and grill for 1 minute on each side. You will need to grill the tentacles for 1 minute longer. Allow to cool, then cut into ¼-inch rings.

Smear the grilled bread with the garbanzo bean paste, then add the marinated beans. Top with the grilled squid, and serve immediately.

On a warm summer evening prior to opening Table 8, chef Neal Fraser and I participated in a Market New Zealand food and wine pairing event at his Grace restaurant in Los Angeles to celebrate our appointment as culinary ambassadors to New Zealand. The heirloom tomatoes were just hitting the farmer's market . . . as were summer truffles aplenty. Looking to highlight, not bury, the natural succulence of the scampi fresh from New Zealand, I chose a light preparation that uses few ingredients: a small batch of farm-fresh tomatoes, a scattering of peppery wild arugula, the best extra-virgin olive oil money can buy, and just a light earthy hint of mild truffle in a shalloty vinaigrette.

New Zealand Scampi /
Heirloom Tomato / Summer Truffle Vinaigrette

SERVES: 8	
DIFFICULTY: Easy	

Finely diced summer truffle	2 tablespoons
White truffle oil	1 tablespoon
Minced shallot	2 teaspoons
Thyme	3 sprigs, leaves only
Chopped flat-leaf parsley	1 tablespoon
Sea salt and cracked black pepper to taste	
Sherry vinegar	1 tablespoon
Juice of 1 small lemon	
Extra-virgin olive oil	3 tablespoons, plus more for drizzling
Heirloom tomatoes	3 different varieties, medium-size, sliced paper-thin
Mixed cherry heirloom tomatoes	1 pint, blanched and peeled (see page 38)
New Zealand scampi	16, split lengthwise, cleaned, deveined, and brushed with extra-virgin olive oil
Arugula, preferably micro or wild, for garnish	

ALTERN8: Substitute large shrimp for scampi one for one.

If heirlooms are not in season, substitute beefsteak or Roma tomatoes.

If summer truffle is too costly or out of season, increase the white truffle oil by ½ teaspoon.

Prepare a gas or charcoal grill.

In a small bowl, place the diced truffle and pour the truffle oil over it. Stir, allowing the oil to be absorbed by the truffle. Add the shallot, thyme, parsley, and a pinch of salt and pepper. Stir in the vinegar and lemon juice and, in a steady stream, slowly whisk in the 3 tablespoons of olive oil.

Arrange the sliced tomatoes, alternating in color, on 8 small plates. Garnish each with a few of the peeled cherry tomatoes. Drizzle with olive oil and season with sea salt and a few turns of the pepper mill.

Season the scampi with salt and pepper, and grill for 1 minute on each side. Place on top of the tomatoes, drizzle with the summer truffle vinaigrette, and garnish with the micro arugula or, even better, wild arugula when available.

This delicate bird can be prepared in a variety of ways, from grilling and braising to deep-frying in tempura batter to pan-searing with a spicy citrus glaze. Here, a straight-up barbecue sauce and grilled corn salsa is all you need. The quail meat retains its subtle gamey flavor but stays light and tender. Remember, a perfectly cooked quail should melt in your mouth.

Barbecued Quail /
Grilled Corn Salsa

SERVES: 8	
DIFFICULTY: Medium	

GRILLED CORN SALSA

Whole ears of corn	6
Unsalted butter	2 tablespoons, soft
Sea salt and cracked black pepper to taste	
Chopped thyme	1 teaspoon
Red bell pepper	1 small, halved, cored, and seeded
Red onion	1 small, peeled and sliced in ½-inch rings
Scallions	1 bunch, tops removed
Jalapeño	1, halved and seeded
Extra-virgin olive oil	½ cup
Limes	2
Chopped cilantro	2 tablespoons
Chopped flat-leaf parsley	2 tablespoons
Semi-boneless quail	8
Barbecue sauce	4 tablespoons

ALTERN8: Blanch whole ears of corn, brush with oil and season, then grill to save time. Please don't use canned!

Prepare a gas or charcoal grill.

To make the salsa, begin by peeling the husks of the corn down from the tip of each ear to the bottom, keeping the husks attached throughout the process. Once all the corn is peeled, remove all the silk and discard. Brush the ears well with the butter; sprinkle with salt and pepper and the thyme. Pull the husks back over the ears of corn, covering as much of the kernels as possible. Using butcher's twine, snugly tie the husks in place. Fill a large bucket with cold water, and fully submerge the corn in the water. Place a medium bowl of water on top of the corn to keep it submerged. Allow the corn to soak for at least 30 minutes.

Place the corn on the grill, turning as needed and not allowing the ears to get too charred. It will take about 20 minutes to cook the corn. Let the corn cool to room temperature. Remove the twine and husks from the corn, and cut the bottom off. Stand the corn up on a cutting board, cut along the cob from the tip down, and remove all the kernels. Set aside.

recipe continues...

Educ8: A Quail's Tale

One of the premier limited producers of farm-raised fowl, Hoffman Game Birds of northern California, delivers some of the finest quail I've ever tasted. The late Bud Hoffman's loyal wife, Ruth, has carried on Bud's labor of love by producing sensational hens and pheasant, in addition to the quail (see Sources, page 252).

Without a doubt, I prefer anything fresh to frozen, but you can also find lightly brined varieties from places like Manchester Farms. If frozen, simply slack them out in the fridge overnight to defrost. When ordering the quail from your local butcher, please specify semi-boneless, meaning the rib cage will be removed but the leg and wing bones will still be attached.

recipe continued...

In a small bowl, toss the bell pepper, onion, scallions, and jalapeño with 1 tablespoon of the olive oil. Season with salt and pepper, and grill until just cooked. Once the vegetables are cooled, cut into a small dice, and place in a small mixing bowl. Add the corn, the juice of the limes, the remaining olive oil, the cilantro, and the parsley. Adjust the seasoning and set aside.

Season the quail with salt and pepper. Place on the grill, and cook for 1½ minutes on either side while basting with your favorite barbecue sauce.

Place a spoonful of salsa on each plate with the quail and serve immediately.

Market abundance often dictates my seasonal menu, and this particular story is a textbook study of ingredient-driven cooking.

This dish began last summer with gazpacho. We had an abundance of tomato seconds generously given to us by Maryann Carpenter of Coastal Organics up north in Ventura County, California. Because our menu was already overflowing with heirlooms, it was natural for us to do something different; in this case, we roasted them on the wood-burning grill with a bed of herbs and additional vegetables. When the peppers, onions, celery, and tomatoes charred up so nicely, a zesty summery gazpacho was a logical next step.

With a grip of Reed avocados just chilling in the walk-in refrigerator from Paul Shaner of Shaner Farms, a chunky salsa came to mind. A little larger in size than the Hass, the Reed has a mellow and sexy flesh that is slightly richer and silkier, but not oily. The avocado combined with watery cucumber made for a nice plump mash against the rustic gazpacho.

What was missing? The heat element. So I roasted a few jalapeños for some green-hot flavor.

Finally, the protein. We started serving this dish with black cod as an entrée, then, for an event, we did the bite-size chicken skewers with the same application—and it worked like a charm. I have to say that as far as chicken is concerned, I'm a thigh man. Once you brine the meat and grill it, you get crispy skins and a pure, deep flavor. Add a dollop of crème fraîche to act as a cooling agent to even the balance, and there you have it: the anatomy of a dish.

Grilled Chicken Thighs /
Wood-Roasted Gazpacho / Avocado Salsa

SERVES: 8 as an appetizer or	
16 for hors d'oeuvres	
DIFFICULTY: Medium	

Chicken thighs	4, deboned, skin removed, soaked in brine for 2 hours, and cut into bite-size pieces (see page 40 for Brine Mix)
Bamboo skewers	16

WOOD-ROASTED GAZPACHO

Oregano	1 bunch
Thyme	½ bunch
Cilantro	½ bunch
Flat-leaf parsley	½ bunch
Ripe tomatoes	6, cores removed
Celery ribs	3, cut into thirds
Head of garlic, split (keep the skins on)	
Red bell peppers	2
Extra-virgin olive oil	7 tablespoons
Salt and cracked black pepper to taste	
Jalapeños	4, roasted, peeled, and diced
Juice of 1 lime	
Red onion	½ small, finely diced

Avocados	2, pitted, peeled, and diced small
Juice of 1 lemon	
Hothouse cucumber	1, peeled and diced small
Chives	1 tablespoon, cut into ½-inch sticks
Chopped cilantro	1 teaspoon
Whipped crème fraîche	¼ cup

ALTERN8: Substitute just tomatoes for the vegetables to make a pure tomato coulis for your saucy needs.

The gazpacho is also guaranteed to make the best Bloody Mary ever.

recipe continues…

recipe continued...

While the chicken is in the brine, soak the skewers and the herbs in water for 30 minutes. Discard the water and reserve the herbs. Once ready, place 1 or 2 pieces of chicken on each skewer, and set aside in the refrigerator.

Preheat a gas or charcoal grill.

In a large bowl, toss the tomatoes, celery, garlic, and bell peppers with 1 tablespoon of the olive oil. Place the herbs on the grill, forming a circular bed. Lay the tomatoes and other vegetables in a pyramid on top of the herbs. Place a large heat-proof bowl on top of the vegetables to seal in the heat. Check on the vegetables periodically as they cook, and remove any that become fully cooked. You are looking for the tomatoes and peppers to be roasted and just slightly charred; the celery should be well wilted and the garlic should be just softening. This should take about 30 to 35 minutes on a medium-hot grill.

While the vegetables are cooking, place the skewered brined chicken thighs on the grill, and remove when fully cooked through, about 2 minutes per side. Allow to cool.

Once the vegetables are ready, remove them and discard the charred herbs. Allow the vegetables to cool. Remove the seeds from the bell peppers, and squeeze the garlic cloves out of their skins. Add 2 tablespoons of the olive oil to a sauce pot and simmer all the vegetables together for 15 minutes.

Prepare an ice bath. Pass the vegetables through a food mill or food processor, season with salt and pepper, and place in the ice bath to cool.

Place the diced jalapeño in a small bowl, and add the lime juice, red onion, the remaining 4 tablespoons of oil, and salt and pepper if needed. Set aside.

In a small bowl, toss the avocado, lemon juice, cucumber, and chive together and mix very lightly with a spoon.

Serve the chicken skewers with the jalapeño vinaigrette and the avocado salsa sides, as well as the chilled gazpacho. Fold the chopped cilantro very gently into the crème fraîche. Add a dollop of the mixture alongside the skewers, and serve immediately.

Melting pot that it is, Los Angeles is blessed with ethnic enclaves where you'll find countless specialty markets. Deep in Koreatown, there's California Market. And just a mile down from Table 8 on Melrose Avenue, there's the Bangkok Market. This is one of Thai Town's best sources for anything from an aisle's worth of dried shrimp (*kung haeng*) and chili paste (*nam prik*) to exotic Thai produce like spinach-esque morning glory and the peppery "lesser ginger," galangal root. Best of all, what would ordinarily be super-expensive at a gourmet food store is a day-to-day necessity for the local Thai population—and that means prices are low!

Another popular ingredient found at the Thai grocer is palm sugar (*nam taan peep*). Raw and unprocessed like honey and made in small quantities, palm sugar can vary in color and flavor from batch to batch, from creamy light beige to a deep brown-gold, from softly sweet to sticky, deep, and rich. Made from the collected sap of the sugar (not coconut) palm tree, palm sugar is boiled in large vessels until it reduces. The final product is allowed to cool into pressed crystalline "cakes" that crumble and dissolve like any other sugar (though it may need some coaxing with a hammer or grater if it's a particularly hard one). Whereas regular processed cane sugar can be painfully sweet, palm sugar takes on a pure, brown-sugary quality. Needless to say, the dentist would advise that small children stay away from it, but I love its complex and slightly smoky, caramel-like flavor. Keep in mind that the deeper the color, the richer the flavor, so adjust the amount of palm sugar accordingly. Wrap up any leftovers and store in a cool, dry pantry.

Grilled Skirt Steak
in Lettuce Leaves / Soy-Ginger Dipping Sauce

Package of bamboo skewers	
Skirt steak	3 pounds, cleaned and trimmed of fat
Soy sauce	1 cup
Juice of 4 limes	
Pineapple juice	1 6-ounce can
Onion	1 small, sliced
Salt and pepper to taste	
Chopped fresh peeled ginger	2 tablespoons
Chopped garlic	1 teaspoon
Palm sugar	2 tablespoons
Rice vinegar	½ cup
Scallions	1 bunch, chopped
Heads of butter lettuce	3
Thai basil	4 sprigs, plus additional for garnish
Cilantro	4 sprigs, plus additional for garnish

ALTERN8: Brown sugar is a last-resort substitution for this dish, second to coconut sugar.

Begin by soaking the skewers in water for 20 minutes to prevent them from igniting when placed on the grill. With a boning knife, trim any visible fat on the skirt steak. Then, cutting on a bias, slice against the grain in 3-inch strips and set aside in a plastic storage container.

For the marinade, combine in a large bowl ¾ cup of the soy sauce, the juice of 2 limes, the pineapple juice, and the sliced onion. Mix well, season with salt and pepper, and pour over the beef. Allow this to marinate in the refrigerator for 1 hour. Remove the beef from the marinade, and skewer with the bamboo.

For the dipping sauce, in a small bowl combine the remaining ¼ cup soy sauce, the ginger, garlic, palm sugar, juice of the remaining 2 limes, the vinegar, and scallions. Check the seasoning, and transfer to a small serving bowl.

Light the grill or preheat the oven to 375°F.

To serve, grill or bake the skewers on a hot grill for about 1 minute on each side, and allow to cool. On a large platter, lay out the butter lettuce leaves, then on each leaf, place a few basil and cilantro leaves. Rest the skewers of beef on the leaves. Have each guest grab a leaf, remove the skewer, and enjoy with the dipping sauce.

I like to think of this as the adult version of the classic child-favorite: peanut butter and chocolate. When you take a relatively basic dense chocolate brownie and doctor it up with a supple, tangy mascarpone mousse to balance and mellow the chocolate, the peanut butter ganache, and all sorts of toasty and nutty fixin's, you get an intense bite of gourmet Reese's.

Mascarpone Peanut Brownies /
Dark Chocolate Sauce / Honeyed Peanuts

SERVES: 8

DIFFICULTY: Medium

BROWNIES

Unsweetened chocolate	8 ounces
Unsalted butter	1 cup (2 sticks)
Sugar	3 cups
Eggs	6 medium
Vanilla extract	2 teaspoons
All-purpose flour	1½ cups, sifted

PEANUT BUTTER GANACHE

Milk chocolate	8 ounces
Unsalted butter	½ cup (1 stick)
Creamy peanut butter	2 cups

PHYLLO CYLINDERS (OPTIONAL)

Phyllo dough	2 sheets, defrosted
Softened unsalted butter, to brush	
Sugar, to coat	

DARK CHOCOLATE SAUCE

Sugar	½ cup
Unsweetened cocoa powder	½ cup
Corn syrup	⅛ cup

MASCARPONE MOUSSE

Heavy cream	1 cup
Egg yolks	4
Sugar	¼ cup
Crème de cacao (optional)	¼ cup
Mascarpone	1 cup

HONEYED PEANUTS (OPTIONAL)

Chopped peanuts	1 cup
Honey	1 tablespoon
Pinch of salt	
Mini chocolate chips, for garnish (optional)	

Preheat the oven to 350°F.

To make the brownies, using a bain-marie or double boiler, in a medium bowl melt the chocolate and butter over low heat, meaning the water is simmering. Remove from the heat and add the sugar, eggs, vanilla, and sifted flour; mix well until smooth. Pour the mixture into a sprayed nonstick 11½ x 16 x ½-inch half sheetpan. Bake for 25 to 30 minutes, or until an inserted toothpick comes out clean.

recipe continues...

For the peanut butter ganache, in a medium bowl melt the chocolate and butter over a bain-marie or double boiler over low heat. Once fully melted, add the peanut butter (still on the heat) and stir until it's super-smooth. Pour over the brownie and place in the fridge to set.

To create the phyllo cylinders for presentation, preheat the oven to 375°F.

Brush 2 sheets of phyllo with butter. Sprinkle with sugar and place the second phyllo sheet atop the first. Brush this sheet with butter. Using two 1½-inch-diameter copper pipes approximately 1 foot long, coat each pipe well with nonstick baking spray. Wrap the phyllo around the pipe. Using the sharp blade of a knife to perforate the phyllo and rolling with your other hand, portion out 3-inch cylinders. Wrap with foil like a candy wrapper, twisting the ends, and bake for 15 to 20 minutes or until the phyllo reaches a deep golden brown. Remove foil, allow to cool, and set aside. Slide each phyllo cylinder off the pipe and store in an airtight container until ready to serve.

For the dark chocolate sauce, combine ½ cup of water, the sugar, cocoa powder, and corn syrup in a small sauce pot over medium heat. Boil for 1 to 2 minutes, stirring constantly, and reserve.

To prepare the mascarpone mousse, whip the heavy cream to medium peaks and set aside. Over low heat in a bain-marie or double boiler, in a medium bowl cook the yolks, sugar, and liqueur, if using, stirring constantly, until thickened and doubled in volume, about 6 minutes. Transfer to a mixing bowl and whip until cool and thickened, 3 to 4 minutes. Fold the cooked egg mixture into the mascarpone, and to finish, gently fold in the whipped cream. Don't work the mascarpone too much, or it will break. Allow this mousse to set up in the refrigerator for at least 45 minutes.

For the honeyed peanut garnish, preheat the oven to 350°F. Coat the nuts with the honey and sprinkle the salt on top. Spread the peanuts onto a parchment-lined sheet pan and bake until just caramelized, watching to make sure that the nuts don't burn, about 10 minutes.

To serve, place the ganache-topped brownie in the center of a plate. Using a pastry bag, fill the phyllo cylinder with the mascarpone mousse, and insert vertically into the brownie. Add a sprinkle of honeyed peanuts and a pool of the rich dark chocolate sauce. Sprinkle mousse with mini chocolate chips, if you like. Serve immediately. If you opt not to make the phyllo cylinders, place a dollop of mousse on the side.

To pull out the refreshing herbal aromatics of the marinated skirt steak and to temper its pungent soy dipping sauce, how about a cooling basil mojito with smooth rum? Quite popular at Table 8 South Beach, this updated old Cuban classic is a food-friendly sipper that gets any barbecue started off on the right foot.

Basil Mint Mojito

SERVES: 1

DIFFICULTY: Easy

Mint	2 sprigs
Basil	2 sprigs
Sugar	1 teaspoon
Soda water	
Juice of ½ lime	
Lime-basil simple syrup (see page 75)	1 teaspoon
Rum	4 ounces

In a tall glass, lightly muddle the mint and basil sprigs with the sugar in a splash of soda water. Add the lime juice, the simple syrup, and crushed ice to fill the glass. Pour in the rum, stir, and top with an additional splash of soda water.

From a chef's point of view,

I always try to bring a savory element into everything I do, from herb-spiked cocktails to a sprinkling of *fleur de sel* on a dessert.

Here, a simple syrup infused with sage makes for one of L Scorpion's most popular tequila drinks. Locally grown pineapple guava (also known as *feijoa*) comes and goes in California for just a fleeting few weeks in November. It makes a terrific garnish as well as an addition to the drink (simply scoop the pulp from the outer shell and muddle with the sage and lime).

A word to the wise: Don't waste top-shelf tequila on your mixed drinks. A 1942 Don Julio will taste pretty much the same as the cheap stuff once you mix in fruit juices and various sweeteners.

Sage Brush

SERVES: 1	
DIFFICULTY: Easy	

Lime	½, cut in two
Sage leaf	
Sage simple syrup (see page 75)	1 teaspoon
Tequila	3 ounces
Pineapple juice	1 ounce
Guava juice	1 ounce
Pineapple wedge or pineapple guava wedge (optional)	

Rim a highball glass with the cut lime. Muddle the lime, sage leaf, and simple syrup in a glass. Pour into a shaker. Add the tequila and the pineapple and guava juices. Shake, and pour into the highball glass. Garnish the drink with a pineapple wedge or, if in season, a wedge of pineapple guava.

The cooling hit of dry champagne makes this the perfect quaff for an afternoon-long lounge with your toes dipped in the pool. It's simple to make this lemony refresher ahead of time and then add the sparkling wine or champagne at the last moment. If you're not familiar with limoncello, the ambrosial liqueur made with sweet Sorrento lemons from the south of Italy, pick up a bottle. It makes a zesty addition when poured over creamy gelato, and gives this sparkling punch a boozy lemon lift.

Sparkling Summer Berry and
Lemon Sangría

SERVES: 8 to 10

DIFFICULTY: Easy

Fresh or frozen berries (raspberries, blackberries)	2 cups
Zest of 2 lemons	
Pink lemonade	6 ounces
Limoncello	4 ounces
Sparkling wine or champagne	2 750-ml bottles, chilled

In a large glass pitcher, mix together the berries, lemon zest, lemonade, and limoncello. Stir and refrigerate for about 2 hours.

When ready to serve, slowly add the sparkling wine to the pitcher, stirring gently with a long-handled wooden spoon. Add ice cubes to white wine glasses, and slowly pour the sangría over the ice, allowing the berries to fall into the glasses.

It's not often that a drink can translate summer's carefree insouciance and long, endless days, but this colorful punch of summer love takes me back to the watermelon seed spitting contests of my youth. Taking on all the big kids, I managed to hold my own and win third place.

If you'd like to give your guests an option to "spike" this nonalcoholic drink, take another watermelon and drill a hole into it. Pour in a bottle of vodka, and allow it to sit overnight. The next day, slice it open and, with a spoon or melon baller, scoop out little pieces of drunken fruit to be served alongside the punch.

Watermellow

SERVES: 8 to 10

DIFFICULTY: Easy

Fresh watermelon juice	8 cups
Fresh orange juice	2 cups
Pineapple juice	2 cups
Fresh lemon juice	½ cup

Combine all the juices in a large punch bowl, and stir together. Chill with ice (at least 10 cups), and serve with vodka-spiked watermelon, if desired.

As the tropical sun goes down over South Beach, the action really heats up, especially at Table 8's lounge, where guests sit sipping drinks underneath ceiling cutouts that reveal the azure-blue pool and sunset swimmers above. People are so open and free-spirited in Miami, and a few of these cocktails, reminiscent of the sunset, definitely keep the party buzzing.

Sex on South Beach

SERVES: 1

DIFFICULTY: Easy

Vodka	1½ ounces
Peach schnapps	1½ ounces
Cranberry juice	1 ounce
Pineapple juice	1 ounce
Orange juice	1 ounce
Splash of Chambord	
Sugarcane swizzle sticks, for garnish	

Fill a highball glass with ice and layer each ingredient, beginning with the vodka on the bottom and continuing with the peach schnapps, cranberry juice, pineapple juice, and orange juice. Finish with a splash of Chambord and a sugarcane stirrer. Serve immediately.

dinner for 8

Shaved Navel
Endive / Beets / Toasted Walnuts / Saint Agur Blue Cheese
Santa Barbara Spot Prawns in Pernod
Tender Bean Salad / Prosciutto / Roasted Tomatoes / Parmesan
Foie Gras–Stuffed Quail / Butter Lettuce and Red Flame Grapes / Meyer Lemon Relish
Baked New Zealand Salmon / Heirloom Spinach / Morel Mushrooms / Pickled Ramp Vinaigrette
Whole-Roasted Colorado Lamb Rack / Pici / Artichoke and Tomato / Salsa Verde
Panna Cotta / Raspberry Coulis

The key to good entertaining is gracefully walking the fine line between convivial host and chef. For a multicourse dinner party, 8 guests is my magic number. I can plan ahead and create a timeline, which means I can actually enjoy my guests. In each recipe that follows, I will show you how easy it can be to execute these dishes with proper planning, so you're not stuck in the kitchen. If you are not planning to serve all 8 dishes at your dinner party, you can serve up combinations of these small plates such as Santa Barbara spot prawns with the Colorado lamb, the tender beans with the New Zealand salmon, or the grilled endive with the lamb.

To kick off the early evening, an easy little mocktail sets the mood. But to turn a dinner party into something truly memorable, select specific wines for each course (like we do at Table 8). This extra step will complement the meal, fuel conversation, and keep the party flowing. And you can be certain that each bite of your creations will be savored with every sip.

This past year, I have had the pleasure of working with Fritz Stuhlmuller to blend signature wines for Table 8. Located just a cork's throw from the Russian River near the romantic town of Healdsburg, the lush and rustic Stuhlmuller Vineyards of Alexander Valley produces some of California wine country's most epic cabernets and chardonnays—and a cruelly small quantity of stunning estate zinfandel. For each course in this chapter, Fritz and winemaker Leo Hansen have recommended some fine wine pairings, all from northern California's wine country.

Some guests walk through the door and a host immediately pops the bubbly. Just because a dinner guest opts for the nonalcoholic doesn't mean that he or she should be relegated to sparkling water with a slice of lime. At the restaurant, we prefer to offer the navel and ask if the guest would like it fuzzy or shaved. The latter is the mocktail of the fuzzy navel, nonalcoholic bliss with summery peach flavors shining through.

Shaved Navel

SERVES: 1

DIFFICULTY: Easy

Fresh-squeezed orange juice	6 ounces
Fresh peach juice	3 ounces
Squeeze of lime	
Slice of orange, for garnish	

Chill the orange and peach juices with the squeeze of lime in a shaker with ice. Strain into a highball glass with ice and garnish with an orange slice.

A perennial crowd-pleaser, the combination of blue cheese, Belgian endive, and walnuts starts a dinner party on an elegant high note. While many salads call for raw ingredients tossed with vinaigrette and served family-style from a giant bowl, here, I plate the course individually. A few additional steps—roasting the red and golden beets separately in coordinating vinegars and toasting the walnuts—will ensure that your guests will be calling you "chef" before the first cocktail is even consumed. I recommend that these two steps be done the day before; you can even preslice the beets to save more time.

Straight from our opening lounge menu, all the classic ingredients commingle freely: the roasted, earthy notes of golden and red beets; tangy-sweet double-crème French blue cheese; the faintly acerbic tang of chicory greens; and the final nutty blast of toasted walnuts bound in a honey-spiked red wine vinaigrette.

Endive / Beets /

Toasted Walnuts / Saint Agur Blue Cheese

SERVES: 8

DIFFICULTY: Medium

Medium red beet	1
Medium golden beet	1
Olive oil	2 teaspoons
Thyme	6 sprigs, plus ½ teaspoon, chopped
Bay leaves	4
Whole black peppercorns	1 teaspoon
Balsamic vinegar	1 tablespoon
Sherry vinegar	1 tablespoon
Walnuts	½ cup
Walnut oil	2 tablespoons
Salt and cracked black pepper to taste	
Honey	1 teaspoon
Red wine vinegar	1 tablespoon
Diced shallot	2 tablespoons
Extra-virgin olive oil	¼ cup
Belgian endive	4
Yellow frisée	1 bunch, cut from the stalk and torn into bite-size pieces
Flat-leaf parsley	8 sprigs, leaves only
Saint Agur blue cheese	4 ounces

WINE PAIRING: **Roederer Estate, L'Ermitage Brut Anderson Valley, Mendocino, 1999**

ALTERN8: **You can use Stilton or Roquefort as substitutes for the Saint Agur blue cheese for a different flavor profile.**

Preheat the oven to 350°F.

Cut either end of the beets so they can stand up, then place in separate small baking pans with 1 teaspoon of olive oil in each. Add ½ inch of water, 2 thyme sprigs, 2 bay leaves, and ½ teaspoon whole peppercorns to each pan. To the red beet, add the balsamic vinegar, and to the golden beet, add the sherry vinegar. Cover each pan with aluminum foil, and roast in the oven for approximately 45 minutes to 1 hour, or until fork-tender.

Toss the walnuts with 1 tablespoon of the walnut oil, the remaining thyme sprigs, and salt and pepper. Transfer to a baking sheet, toast for 10 minutes in the oven with the beets, then discard the thyme and set the walnuts aside.

Dissolve the honey with the red wine vinegar. Add the shallots and chopped thyme and whisk in the remaining walnut oil and the ¼ cup olive oil. Season with salt and pepper.

Remove the beets from the cooking liquid, discard the liquid, and place them in the fridge. Once cool, peel and thinly slice the beets on a Japanese mandoline, keeping them in a nice stack.

Just off-center on each of 8 small chilled plates, fan 4 to 5 slices of beet, slightly overlapping and alternating colors.

Split the endives lengthwise. With a paring knife, carefully remove the core and cut the endives horizontally into 1-inch pieces. Toss with the frisée and the parsley leaves, lightly dress with the vinaigrette, and season with salt and pepper.

Place a small amount of salad in the center of each plate. Brush the beets with some of the remaining vinaigrette, scatter the toasted walnuts, and crumble hearty chunks of the Saint Agur blue cheese on top. Serve immediately.

A "one pan wonder" can be a lifesaver for entertaining. The secret? Have all your ingredients at hand and ready to go. For this appetizer, the preparation is minimal but the flavors are sunny and bright with sweet little cherry tomatoes and a hit of lemon. It's so simple: Sauté the shrimp in the pan and deglaze with Pernod. By doing so, you release all the delicious caramelized bits stuck in the pan—a great beginning for any finishing sauce (especially when you add some pats of butter at the end for richness). Keep in mind, though, that if the bits in the pan cook too long and become darkened, the sauce will impart the same bitterness as the burnt scrapings.

Pernod, an anise-flavored liqueur sipped in Paris cafés as the classic apéritif, is an ingredient not generally utilized in the kitchen. Use it sparingly. The subtle licorice notes, gently heated with a pinch of crushed red chili, play off the plump sweet prawns, the tart cherry tomatoes, and the deep flavor-acid rush of the savory-sweet preserved lemon.

Santa Barbara Spot Prawns
in Pernod

SERVES: 8

DIFFICULTY: Medium

Extra-virgin olive oil	2 tablespoons
Fresh prawns, preferably Santa Barbara spot prawns	8 large, cleaned, peeled, and deveined
Garlic	4 cloves, smashed
Pernod	¼ cup
Fish or vegetable stock	¼ cup
Unsalted butter	2 tablespoons, diced
Quick Preserved Lemon Zest (page 37)	1 tablespoon, julienned
Squeeze of lemon	
Pinch of crushed red chili	
Sea salt and cracked black pepper to taste	
Sweet cherry tomatoes	2 pints, blanched, shocked, and peeled (see page 38)
Chopped fennel fronds (optional)	1 teaspoon

WINE PAIRING: Ferrari-Carano Fumé Blanc, Sonoma County, 2004

ALTERN8: If you are unable to find Pernod, you may substitute a close anisette cousin, Ricard.

You can substitute any North American saltwater shrimp for the Santa Barbara spot prawns.

Does licorice remind you too much of Grandma's bowl of stale candy? If you don't want to impart any anise flavor, just stick with regular white wine or dry vermouth.

Heat a large, heavy-bottomed sauté pan over medium-high heat. Add 1 tablespoon of the olive oil, and at the first sight of smoke, carefully add the prawns. Sear the prawns on one side for 30 seconds. Turn the prawns, add the smashed garlic cloves, and sauté until golden. With no fear, add the Pernod and flame off all the alcohol; this will happen very quickly. Add the fish stock and reduce to half, about 2 minutes. Add the butter and lemon zest, and turn off the heat. Swirl the pan until all the butter is incorporated into a sauce.

Finish the sauce with a squeeze of the lemon, a few flecks of crushed red chili, and sea salt and pepper. Toss in the tomatoes at the last moment, and garnish with a few chopped fennel fronds, if using. Serve immediately.

Educ8: Shortcut for Roasting Garlic

At the restaurant, we have the benefit of prep time in the mornings to get our mise en place ready to go. We roast whole heads of garlic by cutting off ¼ inch from the top and baking them in a covered pan on a few pounds of rock salt until the cloves are cooked through all golden and caramelized, about 35 minutes at 375°F.

If you need to roast garlic on the fly, however, there's a shortcut. Place peeled garlic cloves in a small saucepan. Cover with extra-virgin olive oil and carefully, over medium heat, bring them to a boil until they're evenly golden on the outside. Turn the heat down to a simmer, and allow them to cook through. The whole process will take about 15 minutes, and you can reserve that roasted garlic oil for vinaigrettes, brush it on cooked fish, or serve it as a dip for a crusty baguette.

Ideal for large parties or small, this first course can be tossed, rolled, and plated ahead of time, then dressed and finished à la minute. The simple blanched beans, tossed together with frisée and an easy vinaigrette, get wrapped in whatever prosciutto you choose with long, curled shavings of a seriously good Parmesan cheese. You can also roast the tomatoes a few days in advance and crisp the prosciutto the day before.

Tender Bean Salad / Prosciutto /
Roasted Tomatoes / Parmesan

SERVES: 8

DIFFICULTY: Easy

Prosciutto	16 thin slices
Garlic cloves	3 roasted (see Educ8, opposite)
Whole-grain mustard	2 teaspoons
Sherry vinegar	2 teaspoons
Red wine vinegar	2 teaspoons
Extra-virgin olive oil	¼ cup
Salt and cracked black pepper to taste	
Frisée	2 bunches, white veins stripped
Flat-leaf parsley	8 sprigs, leaves torn
Basil	2 small sprigs, leaves torn
French beans (haricots verts)	1 pound, cleaned, blanched, and chilled
Roasted Tomatoes (page 39)	¾ cup, julienned
Shaved Parmesan cheese, for garnish	

WINE PAIRING: **Seghesio Winery Pinot Grigio, Sonoma County, 2004**

Preheat the oven to 250°F.

Lay 4 slices of the prosciutto on a flat baking sheet and bake until just crisped through, about 10 minutes.

In a mortar and pestle (or food processor), pulverize the roasted garlic into a paste with the mustard. Transfer to a small bowl and whisk in the sherry and red wine vinegars until you reach a smooth consistency. Steadily whisk in a slow drizzle of oil, season with salt and pepper, and set aside.

Toss the frisée, parsley, basil, and beans in a medium bowl. Very lightly dress with the vinaigrette (you may not need to use all that you have made). If you are preparing this dish well ahead of time, do not dress the salad at all and wait until just before you serve.

Lay 8 slices of the remaining prosciutto on a flat surface. Cut the 4 remaining slices in half lengthwise, and use them to increase the width of the 8 slices by slightly overlapping. Divide the bean salad into 8 portions (about a small handful for each), and lay the mix across the lower center of the prosciutto, allowing at least 1 inch of the bean salad to protrude on either end of the ham. Gently and tightly, roll the prosciutto. Slice in thirds and serve with the crisped prosciutto on top, a roasted tomato on the side, and shaved Parmesan as a garnish.

Sounds complicated and fancy, huh? Well, this is a simple dish that will definitely impress.

To many, the richness of a foie gras medallion stuffed into a little quail is the star; but I'm particularly enamored of wilted butter lettuce. Three main varieties of these pale celadon-hued leaves are commonly available at the markets: Bibb, Boston, or Living Butter. My personal favorite and the most delicate of all three, the Living Butter comes in a distinctive clamshell package with the roots still attached. In wilting the greens, you don't really want to kill the living lettuce; just heat the leaves through until soft but not losing their texture. It just takes a couple of seconds.

Pairing the sweet lettuce with the natural sugars of candylike Flame grapes creates a dance on the tongue. But it's the acidic Meyer lemon relish that uses its powers of perfumed sweetness to cut through the richness of the quail love. Try to serve the bird as it just approaches medium, since the bird cooks quickly and all the foie needs is a little warming. Or you can place herb leaves on top of the foie but still under the skin for an optional presentation. However you choose to present it, make sure you order semi-boneless quails, and I recommend that you prep and stuff them the day before and refrigerate overnight.

Foie Gras–Stuffed Quail /
Butter Lettuce and Red Flame Grapes / Meyer Lemon Relish

SERVES: 8

DIFFICULTY: Easy

MEYER LEMON RELISH

Meyer lemons	2
Extra-virgin olive oil	⅓ cup
Diced shallot	2 teaspoons
Diced chives	1 tablespoon
Champagne vinegar	2 teaspoons
Pepper to taste	
California semi-boneless quails	8
Foie gras medallions	8 1-ounce medallions
Salt	
Grapeseed or canola oil	2 tablespoons
Shallots	2 large, thinly sliced
Flat-leaf parsley leaves	1 cup, loosely packed
Verjus or white wine	½ cup
Butter lettuce hearts	2, leaves only
Red Flame grapes	32, sliced lengthwise
Unsalted butter	2 tablespoons

WINE PAIRING: Siduri Pinot Noir, Russian River Valley, Sonoma County, 2003

ALTERN8: You can use regular lemon as a substitute, and any red seedless grape will work in a pinch. The relish can be used for fish, over baby broccoli, or atop grilled asparagus.

For the relish, prepare the lemons by zesting one in long, thin, curly strands over a small sauce pot to catch all those natural oils. Reserve the juice for later use. For the other, carefully segment the lemon by taking a sharp knife and cutting both ends off and thinly slicing around to reveal only the flesh. Slice into the lemon carefully to pop out its natural segments. Set them aside.

Place the lemon zest with the olive oil in the small pot over low heat for 5 minutes. Cool the lemon oil in the fridge. In a small bowl, place the diced shallot, chives, vinegar, and the lemon segments. Stir in the cooled oil, mixing lightly with a spoon. Give the relish a couple of turns of the pepper mill and season with the juice from the zested lemon. Refrigerate until ready to serve.

Preheat the oven to 350°F.

To prepare the quails, using a razor-sharp knife, slice a small hole in the Achilles tendon of one quail leg. Pop the other leg into the hole so

recipe continues…

recipe continued...

the legs are crossed. Stuff a 1-ounce medallion of the foie gras under the skin of the breast cavity.

Cooking in two batches with 4 quails per batch, season each quail with salt and pepper. Heat 1 tablespoon of the grapeseed oil in a medium sauté pan. Place 4 quails in the pan, breast side down, and cook for 2 minutes over medium-high heat. Repeat this process with the second batch, then transfer all 8 birds to a baking pan, breast side up, and bake for 3 minutes for a medium-rare finish. Add an additional minute in the oven if you desire medium doneness.

Drain off the fat from the sauté pan, add the thinly sliced shallots, and cook them over medium-high heat until translucent. Add the parsley leaves and the verjus, then allow the verjus to reduce by half, about 2 minutes. Add the butter lettuce, toss in the grapes and the butter, and season with salt and pepper to taste. Quickly sauté for approximately 1 minute just to wilt and warm the lettuce, then remove from heat. Take the quail out of the oven, place a small nest of the lettuce mixture on each plate (about 4 leaves and 8 grape halves per person), rest the bird on top, and drizzle the cooled Meyer lemon relish around as garnish.

A "baked in a bag" prep, also known as *en papillote*, lends itself well to the dinner party because the presentation of opening that steaming parcel tableside is so dramatic. Yes, it takes a bit of time to prep, including the two hours needed to pickle the ramps in the same method as the pantry section's pickled red onions (page 35), but keep in mind that this dish can be made well in advance with just a quick finishing touch.

When portioning your salmon, keep the fillets consistent in size for streamlined cooking times. This way, you don't have the thin tail finished minutes before, say, the substantial fillet near the head. Prepare the whole salmon the night before so that you can enjoy your party; and remember, the pickled ramps (wild leeks) can also be made weeks prior.

Baked New Zealand Salmon /
Heirloom Spinach / Morel Mushrooms / Pickled Ramp Vinaigrette

SERVES: 8

DIFFICULTY: Medium

Ramps	12, rinsed clean and split in half lengthwise
Flat-leaf parsley	5 sprigs
Extra-virgin olive oil	¼ cup
Olive oil	1 tablespoon plus 2 teaspoons
Unsalted butter	1 tablespoon
Heirloom spinach	1 pound, washed and stemmed
Salt and pepper to taste	
Juice of ½ lemon	
Morel mushrooms	¼ pound, brushed of any visible dirt
Bay leaf	1
Garlic	1 medium clove
Thyme	1 sprig
Fresh salmon	8 4-ounce fillets

WINE PAIRING: Newton Vineyards Chardonnay Unfiltered, Napa Valley, 2003

ALTERN8: Some ingredients seem to magically disappear or go out of season just when you're aching to cook with them. Morel mushrooms are seasonal goodies seemingly straight from Smurfland with a forest-floor flavor that's unlike that of any other wild or foraged 'shroom. Shiitake mushrooms will also work in their place. If ramps are not in season, substitute baby leeks or scallions.

Begin by dicing the ramps and placing them in a small bowl. Pickle them using the same method as the Pickled Red Onions (page 35). When ready, add the parsley, whisk in the ¼ cup of extra-virgin olive oil, and set aside.

In a sauté pan and working in two batches, warm 1 teaspoon of the olive oil and 1 teaspoon of the butter over medium heat. Add half of the spinach and sauté for approximately 2 minutes, until about halfway cooked. Season with salt and pepper and half of the lemon juice. Allow to cool, and repeat with the remaining spinach.

Cut the stems off the morel mushrooms and place in a small pot. Add just enough water to cover the mushrooms by ½ inch. Bring this stock to a boil, reduce the heat, simmer for 10 to 15 minutes, then strain and reserve the stock; discard the stems.

Heat a medium sauté pan to medium-high heat and add 1 tablespoon of the olive oil, 1 teaspoon of the butter, the bay leaf, garlic clove, and thyme. Once the oil has been seasoned, add the morel caps. Sauté the

mushrooms for 2 minutes, fortifying the 'shrooms with the stock, and reduce by half for another 2 minutes. Season with salt and pepper, and allow to cool.

Preheat the oven to 450°F. Cut out eight 10-inch squares of parchment paper.

Fold a crease across the center of each piece of parchment and open it flat again. Looking at the crease horizontally, just ½ inch above center, place a small bed of spinach, then the morels, and finally the salmon. Fold the bottom half over the salmon, then fold the bottom left corner inward 1 inch to form a perfect little right angle. Turn the parcel counterclockwise and tightly fold the right angle over and crease. Continue creasing and turning every 2 inches to create the seal around the salmon. The end result will be a half moon crimped around the edges. Place the prepared salmon portions on a baking sheet, and bake in the oven for 4 minutes. Rotate the baking sheet 180 degrees, then cook for another 4 minutes. The fish should be a perfect medium-rare, and the parchment will puff up and become a light brown as a sign that the fish is cooked.

Quickly present the fish in the bag, then allow the fish to rest for a couple of minutes in front of your guests while you explain how they will open the package. This gives the fish just enough time to steam and complete the cooking process. Show each guest how to open by cutting the top layer of parchment from the flat side of the half moon. Cut around the components, and peel back the parchment (minding the hot steam) to reveal the salmon. Spoon a small amount of pickled ramp vinaigrette on the fish, and enjoy.

The Tuscans are truly masters of unfussiness, and the native foods of this rolling pastoral land aren't complicated with unnecessary garnishing and discordant flavors. The region is not particularly abundant with fish like seaside Cinque Terre or waterlogged Veneto, so heartier, land-based foods find their way into the culinary traditions of the area. Deep in the woods past the winding backroads and in the pastures, you'll find prized T-bone-esque Fiorentina steaks from Tuscany's white Chianina steers alongside wild boar and lamb, a perfect pairing with the region's favorite pasta.

A snakelike, hand-rolled noodle with just three ingredients, *pici* is one of the most classic peasant foods native to Tuscany. Traditionally, home cooks in farmhouses dotting the landscape didn't have the money to purchase precious eggs for their pasta, so this noodle was fashioned out of necessity.

My former sister-in-law's family operate a restaurant in Tuscany, La Fatoria, in Siena overlooking Lake Chiusi. It was on a trip there a few years back that I was served these large spaghettilike coils for the first time. This long and thick, uneven noodle was served with a lovely roasted tomato sauce and some really good extra-virgin olive oil. Its phenomenal texture and beyond-simple preparation make it impossible to forget, especially when paired with the time-honored white wine of Tuscany, that smooth and nutty honeyed Vernaccia di San Gimignano.

Making your own pici is a breeze and can be done a day or two in advance. You can freeze the dough once it's been rolled, pull it out, and boil it up in extra-salted water whenever you have a hankering for culinary rusticity. Serve it with anything from a light Celery Leaf Pesto (page 28) to an olive oil with a sprinkle of real Parmigiano-Reggiano. Tuscans often serve pici with a roasted garlic and fresh tomato *aglione*; here, a moment of purity comes with roasted tomatoes and baby artichokes (easily pan-roasted from start to finish) with a touch of oil and butter. It's really all you need.

Whole-Roasted Colorado Lamb Rack / Pici /
Artichoke and Tomato / Salsa Verde

SERVES: 8

DIFFICULTY: Medium-Challenging

WHOLE-ROASTED COLORADO LAMB RACK

Colorado lamb racks	2
Thyme	8 sprigs
Rosemary	4 sprigs
Oregano	6 sprigs
Bay leaves	12
Garlic	8 medium cloves, smashed
Pinch of cracked black pepper	
Extra-virgin olive oil	¼ cup

PICI

All-purpose flour	1⅓ cups
Extra-virgin olive oil	4 tablespoons
Salt	
Baby artichokes	16
Juice of ½ lemon	
Unsalted butter	6 tablespoons
Extra-virgin olive oil	4 teaspoons
Roasted Tomatoes (page 39)	1 batch
Salsa Verde, for garnish (page 29)	

WINE PAIRING: Stuhlmuller Vineyards Estate Cabernet Sauvignon, Sonoma County, 2001

ALTERN8: You can use canned or frozen artichoke hearts to save time.

Begin by marinating the lamb racks. Wipe off the excess blood from the meat and place in a bowl. Slightly tear the thyme, rosemary, oregano, and bay leaves and add with the garlic cloves, pepper, and olive oil; rub well into the meat. Allow the lamb to marinate for a few hours in the refrigerator.

Make the pici by placing the flour, 6½ tablespoons of water, and 3 tablespoons of the olive oil in a small bowl and, with your hands, stir until well incorporated. You want to knead away from your body, not working the dough too much. Add a pinch of salt, and form the dough into a nice ball and cover with plastic wrap. Allow the dough to rest at room temperature for 15 minutes.

Bring a pot of salted water to a boil.

Cut the dough into four even pieces, then in eighths, then in sixteenths. Roll each out with your hands into long snakes the width of a green bean. You don't need to use flour in this process; the natural elasticity of the noodle will allow it to extend.

Add the remaining tablespoon of olive oil to the boiling water, and cook the pici for 4 minutes. Pass through a colander to drain, toss with just a bit of olive oil, and place in the fridge.

To prepare the artichokes, don a pair of gloves and remove all the tough outer leaves. You will be left with the tender, green-yellow heart. Cut off the very bottom and, peeling the heart down, trim all the way around the green. Cut ½ inch off the top, and split these artichokes in half. In a

recipe continues…

Educ8: Roasting Meats

When cooking for a dinner party, it's far more foolproof to cook a whole rack to the perfect temperature than to individually prepare each lamb chop to each guest's finicky preference. This way, you can sear the lamb off, stick it in the oven, set the timer—and forget about it.

We use both Colorado-style and New Zealand lamb at Table 8. For the Colorado-style lamb used in this recipe, the eye of the rack is large, and the meat is amply marbled. I'm a firm believer that fat equals flavor, but people don't always agree with me. Accordingly, I also serve the leaner New Zealand lamb, which has similar but slightly gamier flavor than the Colorado and has a much smaller eye and more size consistency across the board. Most importantly, meat still needs to rest after being cooked. The resting time allows for the heat and the juices to be distributed evenly, keeping the meat tender. If you pull a roast out of the oven and cut into it immediately, all the blood and juices run out; you end up with a very rare piece in the center that hasn't been tempered properly.

I am a fan of roasting meats with a ton of herbs. To finish the rack with a flourish, you can ignite the herbs to ensure the meat takes on the nuances of the charred aromatics. (Just make sure you're far away from the smoke detector when you do it!)

small sauce pot, fill with water, the lemon juice, and a little salt; bring to a boil. Boil the artichokes for 8 minutes (or you may steam them if you prefer). Turn off the heat, and allow the artichokes to sit for an additional minute. Drain on a paper towel, cut side down, or on a cooling rack.

To begin cooking the lamb, first preheat the oven to 350°F. Remove and discard the garlic from the marinade. Season the lamb liberally with salt. In a cast-iron pan over medium-high heat, sear the lamb (placed back-to-back) for 2 to 3 minutes on one side until caramelized. Flip, and place the herbs on top and place in the oven in the cast-iron pan. Roast the rack of lamb to a nice medium-rare (approximately 115°F) for 10 minutes if you have a New Zealand rack; 20 minutes for Colorado. Take the lamb out and ignite the herbs with a match, allowing the herbs to char, then gently pat out the embers on the meat and tap them off. This infuses the meat with some of their flavor. Allow the meat to rest for at least 15 minutes before you carve.

In a clean sauté pan and working in 2 batches, pan-roast the artichokes by melting 1 tablespoon of the butter with 2 teaspoons of the olive oil over medium-high heat for each batch. Add half the artichokes, cut side down, and cook until caramelized and lightly golden, or about 5 minutes. Try not to move the pan while you cook the artichokes; otherwise, you won't attain the nice color of caramelization. (Note: To save time, you can roast these the day before.)

Pull the pici out of the fridge, and melt the remaining 4 tablespoons of butter with equal parts water in a medium saucepan. Toss the pici quickly and add the roasted tomatoes and artichokes to warm through.

Place the pici in the center of a bowl with the tomatoes and artichokes. Carve the lamb into double chops, and arrange on top of the pasta. Drizzle with the salsa verde.

I'm a purist at heart. For dessert, there's nothing like the "light" and rich flavor of fresh cream and vanilla in a simple panna cotta. One of the most perfect caps to any meal, this closer is all about the jiggle. It doesn't really need a sauce, and sometimes I don't even use a spoon—I just slide it out of the mold into my mouth. I've been known to get cravings and sneak one off the rack in the walk-in cooler for breakfast—and that's before my morning cup of coffee!

Prepare these easy crowd-pleasers a few days in advance. Word to the wise: Be sure to use ice water when it comes to blooming the gelatin sheets; otherwise, the panna cotta won't set up properly and its customary jiggle will be more like a slow-motion shimmy.

Panna Cotta / Raspberry Coulis

SERVES: 8

DIFFICULTY: Easy

Gelatin	2 sheets
Heavy cream	2 cups
Half-and-half	10 tablespoons
Vanilla sugar or granulated sugar	6 tablespoons
Sweetened condensed milk	½ cup
Vanilla bean	1, split
Vanilla extract	¼ teaspoon
Raspberries	½ pint

WINE PAIRING: Arrowood Late Harvest White Riesling, Alexander Valley, Sonoma County, 2001

ALTERN8: Experiment with a different kind of coulis or fruit purée.

Though you really don't need to enhance this basic recipe, there are myriad ways to tweak it out with flavor infusions: Steep whatever herbs you have on hand like rosemary or lavender; steep an Earl Grey tea bag (just be sure to pull it out); add fresh ginger for a little kick.

Soften the gelatin in 4 cups of ice water and set aside.

In a medium sauce pot over medium heat, bring the cream and half-and-half to a boil. Whisk in the sugar, condensed milk, vanilla bean, and vanilla extract. Once the sugar has dissolved, stir in the softened gelatin and allow it to dissolve. Strain the mixture.

Pour the mixture into eight 3-ounce ramekins and refrigerate overnight.

For the coulis, simmer the raspberries in 1½ tablespoons of water for 10 minutes. Adjust the seasoning with a bit of sugar if needed. Purée the berries in a blender, strain, and allow them to cool.

To release from each ramekin (or you may serve it as is), gently place the container in hot water for a few seconds, making sure that the panna cotta doesn't begin to melt. Invert the ramekin onto the center of the plate and drizzle the coulis to your liking.

cre8

secrets of the kitchen

Pomegranate Martini

The Mirepoix

Roasted Sunchoke Soup / Blue Cheese Croutons / Pear

Cress Salad / Duck Prosciutto / Tangerines / Hazelnuts

Grilled Sepia / Clams / Chorizo / White Beans / Salsa Verde

Foie Gras / Beluga Lentils / Onion Soubise / Asparagus / Mushroom Duxelles Toast

Braised Scampi / Roasted Cauliflower / Warm Anchovy Vinaigrette / Toasted Bread Crumbs

Yellowtail / Summer Corn / Parmesan Aïoli / Sungolds and Favas

Kurobuta Pork Loin / Mushroom Grits Cake / Long-Cooked Greens / Braised Bacon

Beef Tenderloin / Oxtail Ravioli / Swiss Chard / Cipollini Onions

Apple Tart / Brown Sugar Sauce / Roasted Apple Ice Cream

If you want to get a taste of what it's like being a Table 8 line cook, tackle these dishes head on. This section includes some signatures and the truly challenging "restaurant-style" menu items that involve multiple components and plenty of advance preparation. And most are finished à la minute, meaning it's all about that crucial time just before serving when everything magically comes together.

Begin by following our philosophy of sourcing out the finest product in its proper season and cooking with a lot of love. Even with a cocktail like the vegetable-friendly mirepoix, experimenting with exotic purple carrots or farm-fresh local baby carrots will keep market-driven cooking exciting. Then there's the moment you walk by the stand overflowing with wild-looking flying-saucer cipollini onions and decide on the spot to prepare some oxtail ravioli and beef tenderloin to go with a golden-roasted batch of these sweet seasonal bulbs. . . . Get some tunes blaring on the stereo, and you'll be well on your way to a successful, delicious evening. Besides, it's fun and rewarding to be chef for the day; to create for friends and family is the most special gift you can give.

Pomegranate Martini

SERVES: 1

DIFFICULTY: Easy

Vodka	2 ounces
Pomegranate juice	2 ounces
Pomegranate molasses	
Pomegranate seeds	8

ALTERN8: You can also make your own pomegranate molasses by slowly reducing pomegranate juice with a pinch of sugar. Use it in marinades or brush on meats like lamb or quail as you're grilling them.

Make a pomargarita by following any basic margarita recipe and adding a splash of pomegranate juice to finish.

Pour the vodka, pomegranate juice, and a drizzle of the pomegranate molasses over ice in a cocktail shaker. Shake or stir, then strain into a chilled martini glass rimmed with the pomegranate molasses. Drop in the seeds as a garnish.

I've always loved the beautiful, sexy pomegranate. When I was growing up in Encino (just outside of Los Angeles), neighbors down the block had a few larger-than-life trees that produced an endless supply of the fruit in the late fall and early winter. They're one of the messiest foods known to man: My mom must have enjoyed washing (or throwing away) my T-shirts after a session with all those ruby-red stains. I'd go straight for the juice, then spit out the remaining seeds.

At the farmer's market, I always look for "splitters"— pomegranates that are so ripe that they crack, burst, and literally split open at the seams. Inside, you get a sneak peek at those glistening red-magenta seeds. Once, at the restaurant, we reached a point of such overflow that we began juicing them and making martinis. And the addition of pomegranate molasses—easily found at any Middle Eastern market or specialty grocery store—makes for a sweet rim to play against this tart and brooding wintry martini.

Mirepoix is normally a diced vegetable base for soups and sauces, but our "liquid mirepoix" combines carrot, celery, and a pickled-onion garnish for a new take on a culinary standard—a drinkable one!

Don't overlook the simple sweet carrot. Especially in California, every farmer has his prized carrot in a wide range of colors and sizes, from Bob Bornt's Holtville, California, BobTops (named for the inch of lopped-off green at the top of this Nantes version) to the squat baby globe. While these varieties are enticing, I usually stick with the regular table carrot available at the farmer's market.

The Mirepoix

SERVES: 1	
DIFFICULTY: Easy	

Fresh carrot juice	1 ounce
Celery juice	1 teaspoon
Vodka	2 ounces
Triple Sec	¼ ounce
Sweet-and-sour mix	½ ounce
Cardamom simple syrup (see page 75)	1 teaspoon
Carrot peel, to garnish	
Cocktail onions	2 pieces, for garnish

Combine the carrot and celery juices, vodka, Triple Sec, sweet-and-sour mix, and simple syrup in a shaker with ice. Strain into a martini glass and garnish with carrot peel and cocktail onions. To garnish, try using pearl onions quick-pickled in the same manner as the Pickled Red Onions on page 35.

We make this soup at the restaurant just as things start to cool down in L.A. (Yes, this actually happens.) It begins with the natural richness of the sunchoke, that delicate root that takes on a nutty flavor once roasted. The seasoned cream adds sexy silkiness, and then there's the classic combination of blue cheese and pear that every chef wishes he or she could take credit for! Add the crunchy texture of a perfectly toasted crouton brushed with walnut oil, and just go ahead and pinch yourself.

Roasted Sunchoke Soup /
Blue Cheese Croutons / Pear

SERVES: 8

DIFFICULTY: Medium

Sunchokes (Jerusalem artichokes)	2 pounds
Extra-virgin olive oil	3 tablespoons
Salt and cracked black pepper to taste	
Heavy cream	2 cups
Thyme	4 sprigs, plus ½ teaspoon chopped
Whole black peppercorns	6
Bay leaves	2
Pinch of crushed red chili	
Baguette	1, sliced on the diagonal into 8 pieces
Walnut oil, to brush	
Onions	2 small, sliced
Garlic	4 cloves, smashed
Dry white wine	1 cup
Bouquet Garni (page 47)	1
Vegetable stock or water	4 cups
Bosc pears	3, cut into small dice
Unsalted butter	1 teaspoon
Poire William or brandy	1 teaspoon
Point Reyes Blue cheese	¼ cup, room temperature

ALTERN8: Substitute Cambozola for the Point Reyes Blue cheese.

Preheat the oven to 375°F.

To prepare the roasted sunchokes, split them in half and place them into a large bowl. Toss with 2 tablespooons of the olive oil and a pinch of salt and pepper, and roast in a covered pan in the oven until very tender, about 45 minutes. Once cooked, reserve a few pieces for garnish.

In a medium sauce pot, add the cream and the 4 sprigs of thyme, the peppercorns, bay leaves, and crushed red chili. Bring to a boil, then reduce the heat and allow to simmer for 30 minutes. Strain and reserve the seasoned cream, discarding the herbs.

For the croutons, brush the baguette slices with walnut oil, then season with cracked black pepper and the chopped thyme. Bake in the oven (while the sunchokes are roasting) until crisp and golden, about 10 minutes.

To prepare the soup, cook the onions in a medium sauce pot over medium heat in the remaining tablespoon of olive oil until translucent. Add the garlic and cook for 5 minutes, then add the white wine and bouquet garni and reduce until all the wine has evaporated, about 5 minutes. Add the roasted sunchokes, then the vegetable stock. Turn the heat to medium low and cook for 30 minutes.

I have a soft spot for the misunderstood Jerusalem artichoke, otherwise known as the sunchoke. Oddly enough, the Jerusalem artichoke is not from Jerusalem, nor is it an artichoke. Botanically speaking, sunchokes are related to sunflowers, while the thistle family claims the mighty artichoke. But the mild and sweet chestnut flavor of this knobby tuber crosses paths with the flavor of the artichoke heart. Legend has it that the name "Jerusalem" was a botched translation of the Italian word *girasole*, meaning "turning toward the sun"—a nod to its sunflower family. Before the colonists settled in America, the sunchoke had already been cultivated widely by Native Americans.

Slice them up raw and use them in salads instead of water chestnuts (you may want to soak them in acidulated water to keep them from browning); boil, roast, or purée them as you would any other root vegetable (they cook quickly, so keep an eye out); and for a happy late-night lounge nibble, fry them up and pair with a smooth, creamy aïoli (see page 23).

Add all but ¼ cup of the diced pears and all of the seasoned cream and cook for an additional 20 minutes, or until the cream coats the back of a spoon. Purée the soup, strain through a fine-mesh strainer, and adjust the seasoning with salt and pepper.

In a small saucepan over medium heat, sauté the remaining pear in the butter for 2 minutes. With confidence, flame with the Poire William, and place the pears in the bottom of each bowl with the remaining sunchokes. Spread the blue cheese on the croutons and set aside. Pour the soup into the bowls, and then top with the croutons.

Sometimes the best ideas emerge from an unlikely mistake. Shortly after the restaurant's opening, I accidentally received a double shipment of Liberty Farms duck breast. Knowing there was no way I'd ever be able to go through that much duck, I decided to preserve some.

Making your own duck prosciutto sounds difficult, right? Not so. Prosciutto is a fancy word for curing, and all it takes is a lot of time for the duck to hang and get nice and dried out. It's ready to use after forty-eight hours and just gets better with time. (You can also find it at specialty gourmet food stores.) Duck prosciutto imparts a slightly more complex flavor than its piggy cousin with that same ethereal texture when it's sliced paper thin. Once I'd prepared the meat, the idea for this salad came to me on its own. It was a natural to pair the cured duck with the tart acidity of the tangerine and the nuttiness of hazelnuts in a wintry salad that satisfies.

Cress Salad / Duck Prosciutto /
Tangerines / Hazelnuts

SERVES: 8

DIFFICULTY: Medium

Kosher salt	½ cup
Sugar	½ cup
Crushed red chili	½ teaspoon
Cracked black pepper	1 tablespoon
Crushed bay leaves	1 teaspoon
Cracked coriander seed	½ teaspoon
Fresh duck breast	2, skin scored if desired
Maple syrup	1 tablespoon
Hazelnuts	½ cup
Honey	1 tablespoon
Fresh chopped thyme	½ teaspoon
Diced shallots	2 tablespoons
Sherry vinegar	¼ cup
White balsamic vinegar	2 tablespoons
Hazelnut oil	¼ cup
Extra-virgin olive oil	½ cup
Truffle oil	½ teaspoon
Watercress	3 bunches
Flat-leaf parsley	8 sprigs, leaves only
Tangerines	4, peeled and segmented

ALTERN8: If you don't have time to make your own prosciutto, swap ¼ pound thinly sliced prosciutto di Parma.

As an alternative to this salad, you can serve your duck prosciutto as you would prosciutto di Parma with traditional accoutrements like fresh sliced melon and good quality extra-virgin olive oil.

To cure the duck, mix the kosher salt, sugar, crushed red chili, cracked black pepper, bay leaves, and coriander seed in a medium bowl. Brush the duck breasts with the syrup, then pack them with the mixture, cover, and refrigerate for 48 hours. Wipe the breasts clean with a dry towel, then wrap in cheesecloth and hang in the refrigerator until needed. You can store the duck for up to two months in the refrigerator.

Preheat the oven to 350°F.

Spread the hazelnuts on a pie plate and toast for about 10 minutes, or until just fragrant. Let the nuts cool, and chop coarsely. For a rustic touch, crack with a heavy-bottomed pan.

For the vinaigrette, in a bowl combine the honey, thyme, shallots, and vinegars, and mix thoroughly. Whisk in the oils in a slow, steady stream, and season with salt and pepper.

Toss the watercress, parsley, and tangerine segments in a bowl. Dress with the vinaigrette and adjust the seasoning. Arrange the greens on a platter, place very thin slices of the duck prosciutto on top, and garnish with a liberal sprinkling of cracked hazelnuts.

By popular demand, this dish always pops up a couple times a year on the Table 8 menu. Created in a vast range of flavor profiles all over the world, from extremely spicy to mild and herbaceous, the simple rusticity of clams in broth can be life-changing for a chef. I've worked with chorizo for a long time in a variety of recipes, but this combination with the sepia (cuttlefish) is a keeper. (By the way, seppie is the plural form of sepia; see page 229 for more information.) I can't get enough of it—and that includes that special touch of "soggy bottom bread" that reminds me of a Cracker Jack prize at the bottom of the box.

Grilled Sepia / Clams / Chorizo / White Beans / Salsa Verde

SERVES: 8
DIFFICULTY: Medium

Seppie	8 ounces, cleaned
Zest and juice of 1 lemon, separated	
Garlic	2 cloves, smashed, plus 1 clove
Oregano	2 sprigs
Thyme	4 sprigs
Cracked black pepper to taste	
Grapeseed or canola oil	2 teaspoons
Chorizo (page 41)	8 ounces
Manila clams	16 medium or 32 small, rinsed
Flat-leaf parsley	8 sprigs, leaves only
Vermouth	4 tablespoons
Fish stock	3 cups
White beans	2 cups, cooked
Salt	
Unsalted butter	2 tablespoons
Crusty bread	8 slices
Salsa Verde (page 29), for garnish	

ALTERN8: Substitute calamari for sepia, the less meaty cousin.

Substitute 6 ounces sliced chorizo links.

Marinate the cleaned seppie with the lemon zest, the 2 smashed cloves of garlic, oregano, thyme, and a pinch of cracked pepper for at least 30 minutes, covered, in the refrigerator.

Preheat the grill.

Add 1 teaspoon of the grapeseed oil to a medium sauté pan over medium heat. Working in 2 batches, add half the chorizo, and without moving it around too much, allow it to caramelize and brown for about 1½ minutes. (Note: If you are not using the chorizo from my recipe, make sure to remove the casing from any other versions.) Add half the clams and half the parsley until it pops and crackles. Pour in 2 tablespoons of the vermouth and reduce by half, about 1½ minutes. Add 1½ cups of the fish stock and reduce by half, about 3 minutes. Toss in 1 cup of the white beans, adjust the seasoning with salt and pepper, and add half of the lemon juice. Add 1 tablespoon of the butter, and let the broth cook down until it gets nice and rich, about 2 minutes. Set aside in a bowl. Repeat with the remaining chorizo, clams, and beans.

On a hot grill, quickly sear the bread, then rub each slice with the remaining clove of garlic (see the Garlic Love Rub on page 52). Grill the marinated seppie for about 1 minute on each side (about 1½ minutes for squid), then cut into ½-inch slices.

Place a crusty bread slice in the bottom of each bowl. Spoon over the clams and chorizo and sprinkle the seppie on top. Drizzle with the salsa verde. Serve immediately.

On a crisp fall evening, nestled amid the smokiness of creamy lentils, the crisp woody earthiness of mushroom toast, and the slightly sweet caramelization of asparagus, a delicate seared medallion of rich foie gras finds its soul.

This preparation involves many steps, so plan ahead and allot yourself a copious amount of time. As in a restaurant, creating the components a day or so before go-time, then pulling everything together à la minute, will ease the pain of doing the dish all at once. Make the onion soubise a day or so ahead of time and simply reheat; ditto for the mushroom duxelles and the lentils.

Foie Gras / Beluga Lentils /
Onion Soubise / Asparagus / Mushroom Duxelles Toast

SERVES: 8

DIFFICULTY: Challenging

ONION SOUBISE

Yellow onions	4, peeled and julienned
Potato	½ large, peeled and cut into large dice
Garlic	4 medium cloves, peeled
White wine	⅛ cup
Unsalted butter	4 tablespoons (½ stick)
Sachet (page 47)	
Salt and pepper to taste	
Sherry vinegar	1 tablespoon, or to taste

BELUGA LENTILS

Yellow onion	1 small, diced
Garlic	4 medium cloves, thinly sliced
Bacon (optional)	1 slice
Extra-virgin olive oil	1 teaspoon
Beluga lentils	1 cup
Bouquet Garni (page 47)	
Salt	1 teaspoon
Heavy cream	1 cup

MUSHROOM DUXELLES TOAST

Unsalted butter	1 tablespoon
Grapeseed oil	1 teaspoon
Diced shallot	2 tablespoons
Minced garlic	1 teaspoon
Button mushrooms	¼ pound, stems removed, finely chopped
Chanterelle mushrooms	¼ pound, stems removed, finely chopped
Shiitake mushrooms	¼ pound, stems removed, finely chopped
Thyme	1 sprig
Bay leaf	1
Ruby port	¼ cup
Chicken stock	½ cup
Salt and cracked black pepper to taste	
Heavy cream	½ cup
Sherry	½ teaspoon
Walnut bread	½ small baguette, cut into 8 thin slices
Walnut oil, to brush	

PAN-ROASTED ASPARAGUS

Jumbo asparagus	8
Unsalted butter	2 tablespoons
Grapeseed or canola oil	2 tablespoons
Thyme	2 sprigs
Garlic	4 small cloves, smashed
Salt and cracked black pepper to taste	
Foie gras	1 pound, cut into 2-ounce medallions

ALTERN8: I've made many versions of onion soubise. It takes an incredibly large number of onions to cook down over the course of an afternoon; it evolves into a deep, concentrated stew that's finished as a purée. You can use red onions or shallots instead of yellow, pour in red wine instead of white. At the restaurant, we serve it with anything from pork loin to wild salmon.

If you have leftover lentils, try thinning them out a bit for a soup that goes from pot to table in about 30 minutes or try serving them with other proteins like baby chicken or lamb.

For the onion soubise, place the onions, potato, garlic, wine, and butter in a large, heavy-bottomed sauce pot and place over medium heat, stirring occasionally, until all the butter has melted. Add the sachet, cover with a tight lid, and reduce heat to low. Simmer for 3 hours. Drain the mixture, reserving the cooking liquid, and discard the sachet.

Pass the onion mixture through a food mill (or potato ricer). Then, place in a food processor and begin to purée, adding back approximately half of the reserved cooking liquid. Season with salt and very little pepper, and finish with the sherry vinegar as desired.

recipe continues…

recipe continued...

For the lentils, in a sauce pot over medium heat, sauté the onion and garlic with the bacon, if using, and 1 teaspoon of the oil until translucent. Add the lentils and bouquet garni, and cover with water by an inch. Bring to a boil, then reduce the heat to low and simmer until the lentils are just cooked, about 25 minutes. About 15 minutes into the 25-minute cooking time, add the teaspoon of salt. You want the lentils to be soft but not mushy.

For the mushroom duxelles toast, heat the butter and oil in a large sauté pan. Add the shallots and garlic; cook until translucent, about 5 minutes. Turn the heat up to high, add the mushrooms, and cook for 10 minutes, stirring constantly. Add the thyme, bay leaf, and port. Flame quickly to burn off all the alcohol, then reduce until dry, about 1 minute. Add the chicken stock; reduce until dry, about 1½ minutes. Add a pinch of salt and the ½ cup of cream, then bring back up to a boil. Reduce the heat to low and simmer for 20 minutes. Finish with the sherry and season with salt and pepper. Remove the bay leaf. Keep warm if serving immediately.

Once the lentils are ready and cooked, drain the remaining liquid and discard the bacon and sachet. Add the cup of cream and simmer for about 10 minutes to make a nice, smooth texture, stirring occasionally. Set aside to cool, or if pressed for time, cool in an ice bath.

Preheat the oven to 350°F.

For the mushroom duxelles toast, brush each of the bread slices with walnut oil and toast on a baking sheet until crisp, 10 to 15 minutes.

While the lentils are simmering, trim the woody ends off the asparagus, about 1 inch, and leave about 4 inches of unpeeled green. Pan-roast in a cast-iron pan over medium-high heat in 2 batches. In each batch, add 1 tablespoon butter and 1 tablespoon oil. Once the butter is beginning to brown, add a sprig of the thyme, 2 garlic cloves, and 4 asparagus spears. Roast for 4 minutes, or until the asparagus are caramelized and cooked through, trying not to move them around too much. Turn off the heat, and allow them to stay in the pan and finish cooking until fork tender. Season with salt and pepper. Repeat with the remaining 4 spears of asparagus.

Finally, score the foie gras, if you like, then place in a hot and dry, medium cast-iron pan. Cook for 2 minutes, depending on the thickness, but making sure not to overcook the liver.

To assemble, smear the toasts with the mushroom duxelles and set aside. Place a spoonful of lentils on the plate and a dollop of soubise next to the lentils. Rest the seared foie gras on top of the lentils, and the asparagus on the soubise. Garnish with the mushroom toast and serve immediately.

I'll never forget my first trip to New Zealand. As culinary ambassador to the country, I was treated to a ten-day journey through both islands, sampling all the idyllic land's finest offerings while on a rigorous itinerary. I must have consumed my weight in New Zealand scampi (known elsewhere as the langoustine). They're among the sweetest and most tender crustaceans of the sea—not as tough as lobster, but with a firm, not dense, texture. It seemed everywhere I went, from the North Island to the South Island, there were pounds of scampi for all. I knew that coming back to Los Angeles, I'd be craving this flawless product. Through my friends at Logan Brown restaurant in Wellington, I made a contact who sends me the pristine tails that are individually quick-frozen (IQF) right there on the boat.

Because it's lodged somewhere between a shrimp and a lobster, scampi is a very versatile shellfish. There are so many ways to prepare one; I like to split it in half with the shell on and brush it with extra-virgin olive oil, then place it under the broiler until just cooked. All you need is a finishing sprinkle of sea salt and a couple of turns of the pepper mill. In addition, it can be grilled (see page 91); I've even had scampi sliced paper-thin in a carpaccio style.

Here, using a simple method, I like an uncomplicated braise in butter for sweet richness. In this variation on the theme of Piedmontese *bagna cauda*, the traditional hot garlic-anchovy butter for raw vegetables, you'll find a "hot bath" for these savory components in the warm anchovy vinaigrette. The briny, salty anchovy plays off the sweetness of the scampi, while the hit of lemon zest cuts through the deep, roasted creaminess of the cauliflower. And don't forget to seal the deal with some crunchy toasted bread crumbs for added texture.

Braised Scampi / Roasted Cauliflower /
Warm Anchovy Vinaigrette / Toasted Bread Crumbs

SERVES: 8

DIFFICULTY: Medium

Cauliflower	1 head
Diced unsalted butter	6 tablespoons, room temperature
Extra-virgin olive oil	½ cup
Onion	½, julienned
Garlic	4 medium cloves, smashed, plus 1 medium clove, chopped
Thyme	2 sprigs
Salt and cracked black pepper to taste	
White wine	½ cup
Chicken stock	½ cup
Bacon (optional)	1 slice
Heavy cream	½ cup
Long zest of ½ lemon, sliced thin lengthwise	
White anchovy	1 ounce, cut in thirds
Juice of 1 lemon	
New Zealand scampi	8 large, peeled and deveined
Toasted Bread Crumbs, for garnish (page 43)	

ALTERN8: Serve with an herb salad of mint, parsley, chervil, chive, and tarragon tossed with a refreshing squeeze of lemon, some olive oil, salt, and pepper.

You can substitute the scampi with large shrimp and prepare in the same manner, or sauté them in a medium pan for 1 minute on each side.

Core the cauliflower and cut into small pieces— mainly florets. In a large sauté pan over medium-high heat, combine 2 teaspoons of the butter and 1 tablespoon of the oil, and caramelize the cauliflower for approximately 10 minutes. Add the onion, the smashed garlic, and the thyme and cook for another 10 minutes. Once they are all evenly browned and fork tender, season with salt and pepper.

Deglaze the pan with the wine, and transfer to a large sauce pot over low heat. Add the stock and reduce for 2 minutes. Add the bacon (if using) and cream, cover with a tight lid, and allow the cauliflower to simmer for 30 minutes. Remove from the heat; discard the bacon and thyme sprigs, and allow to cool. Coarsely mash with a potato masher and set aside, covered, in a warm spot.

For the warm anchovy vinaigrette, in a small saucepan over low flame, melt 3 tablespoons of the butter with the chopped garlic. Add the lemon zest, anchovy, and the remaining olive oil. Simmer for 5 minutes, and adjust the seasoning with the lemon juice, salt, and cracked black pepper. Set aside.

Simmer a large sauce pot of water to 160°F.

In a medium resealable plastic bag, place the scampi with the remaining butter. Push all the air out of the bag and seal. Place in the simmering water and allow it to "poach" for 10 minutes, or until cooked. With tongs, remove the bag from the water, but keep the scampi in the butter.

To serve, place a scampi on top of a small pile of cauliflower in the center of each plate. Drizzle the warm anchovy vinaigrette around the dish, and sprinkle with toasted bread crumbs.

At the height of any season, the abundance of certain ingredients really dictates menu decisions. One fall at the restaurant, I served a salad of fava beans, fresh tomatoes, and wild arugula with some chunked-up Parmesan scattered on top. The following summer, I got in some beautiful local yellowtail (a member of the Jack family related to pompano, and similar to tuna), and I wanted to pan-sear it using the same ingredients in a totally different manner.

Using corn at the peak of the season, we juiced some and decided to make a batch of old-school creamed corn. Then, instead of serving whole fava beans, we gently braised them in olive oil until they softened, which imparts a smoother, creamier consistency than the whole bean could ever achieve on its own. Then there's the rare yellowtail against the cheesy Parmesan aïoli and the slightly tart acidity of bright summery tomatoes. These are the colors of the season: the golds and buttery yellows of the sun. And don't forget the green.

Yellowtail / Summer Corn /
Parmesan Aïoli / Sungolds and Favas

SERVES: 8

DIFFICULTY: Medium

SUMMER CORN

Onion	½, diced
Unsalted butter	8 tablespoons (1 stick)
All-purpose flour	¼ cup
Whole milk	½ cup
Corn kernels	6 cups (from about 8 ears)
Corn juice (see page 152)	¼ cup
Heavy cream	½ cup
Salt and pepper to taste	
Fava beans	1 pound, cleaned, blanched, and peeled
Extra-virgin olive oil	½ cup plus 2 tablespoons
Bouquet Garni (page 47)	½
Garlic	3 small cloves, smashed
Zest of ½ lemon	
Salt and pepper to taste	
Sweet sungold tomatoes	1 pint
Shallot	1, diced
Thyme	Leaves from 2 sprigs, chopped
Yellowtail	8 3-ounce fillets
Grapeseed or canola oil	2 tablespoons
Unsalted butter	4 tablespoons (½ stick)
Thyme	2 sprigs
Parmesan aïoli (see page 23)	½ cup

ALTERN8: Garnish with arugula, shaved or crisped Parmesan, or Toasted Bread Crumbs (page 43); and if you really have some time on your hands, dry out the tomato skins from the sungolds overnight in the oven.

You can substitute garbanzo beans for the favas and mahimahi for the yellowtail.

To make the béchamel for the creamed corn, in a medium saucepan over low heat, sweat the onion in 4 tablespoons of the butter until translucent. Add the flour and incorporate over low heat. Once the mixture is smooth, add the milk, reduce the heat to low, and cook for 20 minutes still over low heat. Strain through a chinois or sieve, and set aside.

To assemble the creamed corn, begin by sautéing the corn in the remaining 4 tablespoons of butter in a medium saucepan over low heat for 5 minutes. Next, add the corn juice and reduce by half over low heat, being careful not to scald the juice, about 1 minute. Add the heavy cream and cook slowly for 20 minutes, stirring regularly over low heat. Finally, add ¾ cup of the prepared béchamel. Cook for an additional 20 minutes over low heat, stirring often. Remove from the heat, season with salt and pepper, and reserve. You will want to reheat just before serving.

Reserving a small amount of favas for garnish, add the beans to a small pot and cover with the ½ cup of olive oil. Place the bouquet garni and garlic in the pot, and add the lemon zest. Slowly bring this mixture to a gentle boil and immediately reduce the flame to low. Cook the beans until they are soft, about 25 minutes, but be careful not to cook them over a high heat or they will become discolored. You want the beans to be just a bit beyond fork tender.

recipe continues...

Educ8: Corn Juice

To make corn juice, take ½ cup of kernels and place in a blender with a few drops of water. Purée, then strain.

Educ8: Are Fava Beans Really Vicious?

Fava beans, or broad beans, are one of those vegetables that instill a fair amount of fear in the average person. (At least, that's what I've been told by diners over the years.) Many customers are unfamiliar with or intimidated by this native bean of Europe. *Vicia faba* was *the* bean of Europe back in the day and has discovered a stateside resurgence here in the New World.

I use favas frequently at the restaurant when they are available, usually from early spring to early summer. They can be a bit labor-intensive and expensive to begin with, but they're totally worth it, especially in this preparation.

recipe continued…

Pull out and discard the bouquet garni, lemon zest, and garlic clove. Drain the beans from the oil, and remove to a bowl, reserving the oil for later use. Using a potato masher, mash up the beans, adding a bit of the cooking oil as needed to achieve a chunky, rustic spread. Season with salt and pepper, and set aside.

For the tomatoes, bring a small pot of salted water to a boil, then quickly blanch the tomatoes and shock them in an ice-water bath to refresh them. Peel the tomatoes, and place them in a small bowl. Add the shallot and chopped thyme, a few turns of the pepper mill, and the remaining 2 tablespoons of olive oil and toss lightly. Set aside.

Season the fish with salt and pepper. In a cast-iron pan over medium to high heat (which should be very, very hot) and working in 2 batches, add 1 tablespoon of the grapeseed oil and 4 of the fish fillets to the pan. Sear on one side for 3 minutes, reduce the heat to low, and, using a dry, damp towel, wipe away the discolored oil from around the fish fillets in the pan. Add 2 tablespoons of the butter, a sprig of the thyme, and a garlic clove. With a spoon, tilt the pan and baste the raw side for about a minute with the melted butter and oil until the fish is medium rare to rare. Allow the fish to rest for 2 minutes and cut into bite-size medallions. Repeat with the remaining fish.

Spread a fair amount of the chunky fava spread just off the center of a small plate. Spoon the corn directly next to the purée. Fan the yellowtail on top of the vegetables, then dollop with the Parmesan aïoli. Garnish the plate with a few marinated tomatoes and the remaining favas.

Every now and then, there's a dish that comes to me in the form of a theme. Here, it's pork. It just so happened that we had some beautiful collard greens that we picked up at the Wednesday Santa Monica farmer's market. We had the Kurobuta pork loin brining for twenty-four hours (but all you need for this recipe is overnight!) and a ham hock jus (which had been simmered for what feels like forever) in the kitchen. Since I was leaning in a down-home southern direction for the dish, it made sense to run out and buy some grits, something you don't see on L.A. menus too often. Loving that Kurobuta pork, I was going to fortify every element with more pork, so that's how the braised bacon snuck in there. If you're so inclined, feel free to pick the meat from a ham hock and finish the grits with them to really pig out!

Kurobuta Pork Loin / Mushroom Grits Cake /
Long-Cooked Greens / Braised Bacon

SERVES: 8

DIFFICULTY: Challenging

LONG-COOKED GREENS

Olive oil	½ cup
Onion	1, julienned
Garlic	2 cloves, cracked
Bacon (optional)	2 slices
Chili de arbol	1 pod, dried
Bay leaf	1
Collard greens	4 bunches, cleaned

BRAISED BACON

Bacon slab	10 ounces
Spice Mix (page 63)	
Salt to taste	
Extra-virgin olive oil	1 teaspoon
Onion	½ small, sliced
Garlic	2 cloves, smashed
Thyme	2 sprigs
Bay leaves	2
White wine	⅛ cup
Chicken stock	½ cup

MUSHROOM GRITS CAKE

Unsalted butter	4 tablespoons (½ stick)
Onion	½ small, diced
Chopped garlic	½ tablespoon
Grits	½ box (3½ ounces)
Mushroom stock or water	8 cups
Button mushrooms	½ cup, thinly sliced
Grated Cheddar cheese	¼ cup
Salt and pepper to taste	
1 boneless Kurobuta pork loin	2 pounds, brined overnight (see pages 40 and 157)
Onion	½, julienned

Preheat the oven to 350°F.

To prepare the long-cooked greens, in a large sauce pot over medium-high heat, add the olive oil and slowly sweat the onion, garlic, bacon (if using), chili pod, and bay leaf until the onion and garlic are translucent, about 5 minutes. Add the greens in batches, allowing them to cook down as you go. Once the greens have been incorporated, reduce to a simmer. Cover with a lid and cook until very tender, about 2 hours, stirring occasionally. Remove the bacon, if using, the chili pod, and the bay leaf.

For the braised bacon, score the skin of a 10-ounce slab. Sprinkle liberally with spice mix and salt. In a hot sauté pan on medium, heat the oil. Place the bacon in the pan, skin side down, and press down for 2 minutes, reducing the heat as the bacon caramelizes. With the flame still lowered, flip the slab, repeating the same process. Keeping the bacon still in the pan, wipe out the excess fat, then add the onion, garlic, thyme, and bay leaves. Sauté until translucent, about 30 seconds. Add the white wine and reduce by half, approximately 1 minute. Add the chicken stock, raise the heat to high, and when it comes to a boil, tightly cover the pan with 2 layers of foil. Place in the oven. Cook for 75 minutes, then remove the foil lid and finish for another 15 minutes. Allow the braised bacon to rest in its own juices until it reaches room temperature. Carefully transfer to a platter. Strain the juices and keep warm.

recipe continues...

Educ8: Collard Greens

Ever-so-nutritious collard greens don't find much popularity outside of the Deep South and Texas. My guess why? Many people don't know what to do with them. If you put them in a pot, set it, and forget it, you'll find that the longer you leave it on a low flame, the more the bitter flavor of the raw leaves diminishes and the more serious depth the dish takes on. These aren't just a bunch of greens that you're stripping off a rib; they become a little pot of love.

Many Table 8 regulars habitually order a side of collards in addition to their entrée. And the possibilities for accompaniment are endless, from braised meats to hearty fish dishes. Break down the childhood "eat your greens" phobia and give them a try.

recipe continued...

To prepare the mushroom grits cake, melt the butter in a large uncovered sauce pot and sauté the onion and garlic until translucent, about 10 minutes. Next, add the grits and toast well over low heat. Add the first 4 cups of stock and the mushrooms and cover. Stir frequently and cook over low heat for 30 minutes. Add the remaining stock and continue to cook, covered, over low heat for about 15 minutes, stirring frequently. Once the consistency of a soft polenta is reached, stir the Cheddar cheese into the grits and season with salt and pepper.

Prepare a small rimmed baking sheet with nonstick spray, and spread the mixture onto the pan. Refrigerate the grits cake so it will set, then cut into individual portions with a cookie cutter for round cakes and reheat when ready to serve.

Preheat the oven to 400°F.

Pull the Kurobuta loin from the brine, and rinse in cold water. In a cast-iron pan over medium-high heat, place the scored loin skin side down and pan-roast until it begins to caramelize. Flip after 4 minutes, cook for 4 minutes on the other side, then cook it an extra 1 minute to really seal in the juices. Turn the heat off and remove the loin for just a moment. Wipe out the pan with a damp kitchen cloth. Place the julienned onion in the middle like a little nest, place the pork back in on top, and bake uncovered for 35 minutes (or until it reaches an internal temperature of 120°F). Allow the meat to rest, then slice into 8 servings.

To assemble, place a mushroom grits cake on each plate, followed by a portion of the long-cooked collards. Add the slice of Kurobuta loin and top with the thickly sliced braised bacon and a drizzle of bacon jus. Serve immediately.

Educ8: Hog Wild for Kurobuta Pork

For me, the discovery of Kurobuta pork was love at first bite. After sampling this domestic "varietal," I've never been able to go back to generic pork. No matter what you do with it (even accidentally overcooking it), you'll still end up with an incredible finished product.

According to food lore, English statesman Oliver Cromwell and his stationed troops discovered a delicious purebred hog from the shire of Berks in England about three and a half centuries ago. The hogs were later given as a diplomatic gift to the Japanese in the nineteenth century. In Japan, the special heirloom breed of Japanese black hog was named Kurobuta. All Kurobuta is by definition 100 percent Berkshire hog, and recently a handful of elite farms in the United States have started producing it. Our Kurobuta comes from Snake River Farms in Idaho (snakeriverfarms.com).

Look at the pork itself in its raw state. You can tell by the color of the meat that it's richer, a little darker, and marbled with supple fat, like a fine steak. And once it's cooked and you cut into it, you'll see the gleaming juices streaming from the meat itself. This is the Rolls-Royce of the pork world.

It's "rare" that we serve filet mignon at Table 8; generally speaking, I like to use different cuts of meat that have a bit more character than the old passé beef tenderloin. However, we created this dish for a New Year's Eve menu with an oxtail ravioli that adds the richness and depth that the tenderloin can lack on its own.

Just to dispel a myth, oxtail is by no means the tail of an ox. Maybe it started off that way, but basically, now it's the cattle tail. Years ago, it was probably the butcher's cut (the piece the butcher takes home) or a bistro cut (normally served in lower-end restaurants), but in the past fifteen years or so, it has found its way into finer dining establishments. Chefs take advantage of its richness and nuance, sometimes adding oxtail to stocks for extra gelatinous character.

Always look for a two-inch cut, and be sure to trim a fair amount of the fat layer prior to cooking or braising. There's nothing like walking by a braising pan that's recently been pulled from the oven and grabbing one of those perfect, glistening nuggets of sticky, deeply caramelized oxtail.

Beef Tenderloin / Oxtail Ravioli /
Swiss Chard / Cipollini Onions

SERVES: 8

DIFFICULTY: Challenging

Grapeseed or canola oil	4 teaspoons
Oxtail	6 medium 2-inch cuts, trimmed of fat
Salt and cracked black pepper to taste	
Celery	½ rib, cut into ½-inch pieces
Carrot	½, cut into ½-inch pieces
Garlic	5 medium cloves, smashed
Onion	½ small, cut into ½-inch slivers
Red wine (cabernet sauvignon)	½ cup
Bouquet Garni (page 47)	
Beef stock	2 cups
Celery	½ rib, finely diced
Carrot	½ medium, finely diced
Yellow onion	½ medium, finely diced
Fresh pasta sheets	24 6-inch (½ pound)
Cipollini onions	½ pound
Kosher salt	1 pound
Thyme	4 sprigs
Bay leaves	4
Whole black peppercorns	1 teaspoon
Olive oil	1 tablespoon
Swiss chard	2 bunches
Unsalted butter	1 tablespoon
Diced shallot	2 teaspoons
Beef tenderloin	8 3-ounce medallions

Preheat the oven to 300°F.

In a heavy-bottomed sauce pot, heat 1 teaspoon of the grapeseed oil over medium-high heat. Season the oxtails with salt and pepper, then caramelize all sides for about 2 minutes per side. Remove from the pan and set aside; discard the oil. Add another teaspoon of oil; add the celery and carrot pieces, garlic, and onion; and sauté together until golden brown, about 6 minutes, stirring constantly. Deglaze the pan with the cabernet, add the bouquet garni, and reduce until all the wine has evaporated, about 2 minutes. Place the seared oxtail back in the pot, add the beef stock to cover the oxtails by at least half, and bring to a boil. Cover and place in the oven. After 1 hour, remove the lid and very carefully turn the oxtails so the part that wasn't submerged is now covered. Replace the lid and cook for another 1½ hours. Remove the lid.

Continue to cook the oxtails, basting every 10 minutes until the meat is easily removed from the bone, or approximately 30 to 45 minutes. Once fully cooked, remove from the oven. Using a ladle,

recipe continues...

skim as much fat off the top as you possibly can and discard. Allow the oxtails to cool at room temperature in their own juices; this will really lock in the flavor and create tender meat. Once the oxtails are completely cool, remove from the juice and set aside. Strain the liquid through a fine-mesh strainer into a small sauce pot. Allow the fat to settle, and skim once again. Turn the heat to medium and allow the liquid to reduce by half, about 10 minutes. Set aside.

With your hands, pick all the meat off the tail bones, and set aside to cool. Toss the bones and any fat or cartilage.

In a small sauté pan, heat 1 teaspoon of the grapeseed oil over medium heat. Sauté the finely diced celery and carrot for 1 minute, add the yellow onion, and cook for 2 minutes, stirring occasionally. Once the vegetables are cooked through, transfer to a medium bowl. Add the picked meat to the vegetables, and stir in just enough of the braising liquid to bind the mixture (approximately ¾ cup), reserving the rest. Adjust the seasoning with salt and pepper, and allow this ravioli filling to cool.

Lightly dust a prep surface with flour. Lay a pasta sheet on top, and place 1 heaping tablespoon of filling per raviolo 2½ inches apart. With a basting brush, brush around the filling with a little water, and place the second sheet on top. Using the palm or side of the hand, get all the air out of each raviolo, tightly forming the pasta to the filling. Cut out with a 3-inch square or 80-millimeter ring mold. At this point, you can freeze them for 2 weeks or boil them up right away in salted water for 2 minutes or until they float to the top. Cook the ravioli just before serving the meal.

Next, to prepare the cipollini onions, preheat the oven to 400°F.

Place the kosher salt, herbs, and peppercorns in a large ovenproof sauté pan. Toss the onions in a small bowl with the olive oil, then transfer to the pan. Cover with foil, and bake in the oven for 45 minutes to 1 hour. The onions should be golden in color and soft to the touch. Allow the onions to cool, and reserve the salt for another roasting. Cut the root end off each onion, and squeeze from the top to pop out that sweet roasted center. Set aside.

For the Swiss chard, boil a large enough pot of salted water for blanching the greens. With a paring knife, cut the stem out of the chard leaves, then cut the stems into 2-inch-long ribs, and then into ¼-inch-wide strips. First, cook the stems until tender, about 2 minutes, and refresh them in an ice-water bath. Repeat with the leaves. Melt the butter in a sauté pan, add the shallots, and cook them until translucent. Add the chard, and cook until heated through. Season with salt and pepper.

Finally, season the beef medallions well with salt and pepper. Sear them in the remaining teaspoon of grapeseed oil in a cast-iron pan over medium-high heat for 2 minutes on each side for a nice medium rare.

In the center of each plate, place a small amount of Swiss chard leaves with some chard stems to the right. Lay the beef on top of both, with the oxtail ravioli on top of the beef and cipollini onions scattered about. Serve immediately.

Educ8: Braise Patiently

Directly proportionate to the love you give it, braising transforms a less-than-ordinary piece of meat into something really special. It's the nurturing that's involved—the slow cooking, the basting, the time—that makes me a loyal fan of this technique. If you're marinating or braising, start the dish the day before so you have plenty of time to get the show on the road. It's all about patience while braising, but after all that time, the big payoff is massive flavor. One of the keys to this method is allowing the meat time to rest and to cool down to room temperature in the braising liquid. It's a slow boil to bring it up; bring it down the same way. Don't rush it.

There's nothing more all-American than an apple pie (and possibly nothing more French than a tarte Tatin). Somewhere in between the two, this two-day apple tart deconstructs the classic elements: a rustic and gooey crustless "tart"; gingery, buttery crumble; a crisp cinnamon dough cookie; a drizzle of caramelized brown sugar sauce. All that's left? Serving it à la mode with roasted apple ice cream (using all the decadent drippings from baking the apples). The tart must sit overnight before baking, and your ice cream maker must be ready to go the day-of, so make sure to stay organized with plenty of time on your hands for this dessert. But in the end, when your guests have experienced confectionary ecstasy, you'll know it was worth the effort.

Apple Tart / Brown Sugar Sauce
/ Roasted Apple Ice Cream

SERVES: 8	
DIFFICULTY: Challenging	

APPLE TART

Braeburn or Jonagold apples	7
Granny Smith apples	7
Unsalted butter	⅓ cup plus 1 tablespoon, melted
Granulated sugar	¾ cup
Pinch of salt	
Vanilla extract	1 teaspoon

CINNAMON DOUGH COOKIE

Unsalted butter	1¼ pounds (5 sticks), room temperature
Confectioners' sugar	1 cup
Egg yolks	6
Calvados	2 tablespoons
All-purpose flour, sifted	6¼ cups
Baking powder	1 tablespoon
Ground cinnamon	¼ cup

GINGERBREAD CRUMBLE

Brown sugar (dark or light)	1 cup
Unsalted butter	1 cup (2 sticks), room temperature
Almond flour	¾ cup
All-purpose flour	1 cup
Ground cinnamon	½ teaspoon
Ground nutmeg	¼ teaspoon
Ground ginger	½ teaspoon
Pinch of salt	

ROASTED APPLE ICE CREAM

Heavy cream	2 cups
Whole milk	2 cups
Vanilla bean	1, split
Granulated sugar	1 cup
Egg yolks	15
Apple trimmings from tart	2 cups

BROWN SUGAR SAUCE

Light brown sugar	½ cup, lightly packed
Honey	1 tablespoon
Heavy cream	2 cups

recipe continues...

To prepare the apple tart, begin the day before by peeling the apples and slicing them with a mandoline. Place them in a large bowl and add the melted butter, granulated sugar, salt, and vanilla extract and mix until thoroughly incorporated. Spread the apple mixture evenly onto a parchment-lined sheet pan, and place a heavy pot or stacked sheet pans over the top. Allow this mixture to sit overnight in the refrigerator, using a larger sheet pan on the bottom to collect all the drippings.

Also the day before, make the cinnamon dough by creaming the butter and confectioners' sugar in the mixer, then adding the egg yolks and Calvados. Sift together the all-purpose flour, baking powder, and cinnamon. Add the flour mixture to the butter-egg mixture, and mix until incorporated. Chill in the refrigerator for a few hours.

Preheat the oven to 350°F.

Roll out the cinnamon dough and, using an 80-millimeter round cookie cutter, cut into shapes. Bake on a greased baking sheet until just golden, about 10 minutes. Cool on wire racks. Store in an airtight container until ready for use.

Continue the day before by making the gingerbread crumble, and begin by preheating the oven to 350°F.

Cream together the brown sugar and butter in a medium bowl. In a separate small bowl, sift together the almond flour and all-purpose flour with the cinnamon, nutmeg, ginger, and salt. Add to the sugar and butter; mix well until it forms a cookie dough consistency. Pass the dough through a cooling rack to create large "crumbles" on top of a sheet pan. Bake on a greased sheet until golden, about 15 to 20 minutes. Allow to cool before splitting into rustic crumbly chunks. Store in an airtight container until ready for use.

The next day, preheat the oven to 325°F.

Bake the crustless apple tart for 3½ hours with the same sheet pan below it, covered in foil, to collect the drippings. You will need to reserve them for the roasted apple ice cream, so do not discard. Refrigerate the tart until ready to use.

Prepare the ice cream first by making a basic custard: Heat the cream and milk over medium-high heat in a medium saucepan, and steep with the vanilla bean.

In a separate bowl, whisk the sugar with the egg yolks until just incorporated. Once the cream mixture has boiled, drizzle it slowly into the egg yolks to temper them, whisking as you go. Place the mixture back on the stove and cook over low heat until the mixture thickens slightly and coats the back of a spoon. Remove the vanilla bean. Add the apple drippings to the saucepan, then blend with a hand blender until smooth, strain through a fine-mesh sieve, and immediately place the saucepan in an ice-water bath. When the custard is cool, freeze according to the directions for your ice cream maker.

To make the brown sugar sauce, in a small saucepan over medium to high heat, dissolve the brown sugar into the honey, stirring, approximately 5 minutes. Though the mixture will gain some color, make sure it doesn't burn. Slowly whisk in the cream and allow the sugar to continue to dissolve. Cook over medium heat until the sauce evenly coats a spoon but does not boil over, approximately 7 minutes.

To plate, once the apple tart is cooked and cooled, use an 80-millimeter ring mold to cut out shapes. Use the cinnamon dough cookie as the base for the roasted apples. If you like, sprinkle granulated sugar on top of the tart and caramelize with a kitchen torch. Sprinkle with gingerbread crumble, and drizzle the brown sugar sauce around. Serve à la mode with the roasted apple ice cream.

s8

comfort foods

Mini Onion Soup

Warm Winter Greens / Sweet Gorgonzola / Quince Vinaigrette

Smoked Sturgeon / Poached Egg / Olive Oil Croutons / Red Wine Vinaigrette

Braised Chicken Oysters Piccata

Lamb Osso Buco / Saffron Risotto Milanese

Warm New Potatoes / Melted Brie / Baby Arugula

Charred Baby Broccoli / Marinated Peppers / Warm Anchovy Vinaigrette

Carrot Cake / Cream Cheese Mousse

Noggin' It

Table 8 Creamsicle

Cranberry Fruit Cocktail

Indian Summer Punch

After cooking in San Francisco for a couple of years, I returned to my hometown, L.A., but I try to travel to northern California whenever possible. Once a year, I take my sisters with me to California wine country (which has become a really cool family tradition). Most recently, we stayed at the Stuhlmuller family's vineyard in the Anderson Valley. Those chilly evenings inspired me to create hearty and comforting small plates. There, the warm winter greens salad set against a backdrop of rolling deep-green vineyards felt appropriate for the season. And there's nothing like a piece of succulent braised lamb osso buco resting comfortably atop a tried-and-true saffron-laced risotto. Or the crusty, cheesy warmth from a perfectly prepared onion soup eaten with a blazing fire in the background, surrounded by good friends and family, and while enjoying flights of delicious vintages.

After dinner, we bundled up in heavy jackets and headed up the hill behind the main house. I'll never forget the midnight boccie blowout and impromptu concert with my sisters singing and dancing under the stars. Ah, the magic of good wine.

One of the signature comfort soups of all time: onion soup gratinée. There's something inherently soul-satisfying and rustic about gobs of bubbling cheese atop crusty bread floating on a broth of deeply caramelized sweet onions.

Though many recipes call for red or white wine, I've always used beer to make this dish; the hops and malt play off the nuttiness of the cheese and the stewed onions. This may seem like a lot of onion for not a lot of soup, but onions lose about three quarters of their volume as they cook down. As for the beer, I like to use a full-bodied dark beer such as Anchor Steam Ale. Go for a nice handcrafted microbrew, and you'll be pleased you did.

Mini Onion Soup

SERVES: 8	
DIFFICULTY: Easy	

Unsalted butter	4 tablespoons (½ stick)
Onion	4 medium, julienned
Garlic	4 medium cloves, thinly sliced
Salt	
Brown sugar	1 tablespoon
All-purpose flour	2 teaspoons
Dark beer	1 12-ounce bottle, preferably ale
Bouquet Garni (page 47)	
Dried thyme	½ teaspoon
Beef stock	8 cups
Cracked black pepper to taste	
Baguette	½, cut into ⅜-inch slices and toasted
Grated Surchoix Wisconsin Gruyère cheese	1 cup
Grated Parmesan cheese	¼ cup

ALTERN8: Experiment with different kinds of beer or ale—the darker the better—for different flavor profiles.

In a large soup pot, melt the butter over medium-high heat. Add the onions, garlic, and a pinch of salt and begin to cook down, stirring frequently. Cook until the onions become very tender, about 30 minutes. Add the brown sugar and continue to cook until the onions are nicely caramelized, about 10 minutes. Add the flour and stir constantly for 2 minutes. Pour in the beer, add the bouquet garni and thyme, and reduce by half, about 3 minutes. Add the stock, bring to a boil, and then reduce to low heat and simmer for 30 minutes. Adjust the seasoning with salt and pepper.

Preheat the oven to 450°F.

Ladle the soup into small, ovenproof soup crocks. Float a couple of pieces of the toasted baguette on the soup, and top generously with the cheese. Place the crocks on a baking sheet and bake in the oven for 10 minutes, then place under the broiler until the cheese is golden and bubbling.

In the winter months when chicories are abundant, it's nice to have a colorful warm salad appetizer. Here, a lightly wilted emerald-green salad with rich cheese gets perked up with sexy quince-balsamic vinaigrette.

For bitter greens, it's all about using a sweet foil—from the creamy sweetness of the Gorgonzola dolce to the dense, candylike quince. Try to experiment with different cheeses and greens, depending on what's in season and available at the market: for greens, a dandelion green or pointy Italian puntarelle from Lazio; for cheeses, a Maytag blue for crumbly garnish or sharp Cabrales for a more pungent hit of blue-cheese tang.

Warm Winter Greens /
Sweet Gorgonzola / Quince Vinaigrette

SERVES: 8	
DIFFICULTY: Easy	

Quince paste (membrillo)	4 ounces, cut into small pieces
Balsamic vinegar	½ cup
Extra-virgin olive oil	½ cup plus 4 teaspoons
Salt and cracked black pepper to taste	
Belgian endive	2, cored and sliced crosswise
Escarole	1 head, inner leaves torn into bite-size pieces and outer leaves discarded
Frisée	2 small heads, torn into bite-size pieces
Radicchio	1 small head, torn into bite-size pieces
Garlic	4 medium cloves, smashed
Gorgonzola dolce	4 ounces, crumbled

In a food processor or blender at a low setting, purée the quince paste with ¼ cup water and ¼ cup of the balsamic vinegar. Slowly drizzle in ½ cup of the olive oil and process until fully emulsified. Place in a small bowl and season with salt and freshly cracked black pepper.

Put the endive, escarole, frisée, and radicchio in a large bowl and mix thoroughly. Divide into 4 batches for sautéing. Heat 1 teaspoon of the olive oil in a large sauté pan. Add 1 of the garlic cloves and over medium-high heat, cook until the garlic is golden brown, or about 4 minutes. Discard the garlic. Add one quarter of the greens to the oil and sauté for about 1 minute, allowing the greens to get a bit of color. Add 1 table-spoon of the balsamic vinegar, season with salt and pepper, and remove from the pan. Repeat this process three additional times.

Arrange the greens on a platter or in a large bowl. Drizzle the vinaigrette around the warm greens, crumble the Gorgonzola dolce on top, and serve while still warm.

Swap smoky sturgeon in lieu of bacon to give the country French *frisée aux lardons* salad an updated twist. With its amber-colored skin and meaty, buttery flesh, the smoked fish makes for an ambrosial savory spin at your next picnic-style brunch.

If Peter Shaner has them on hand, we use duck eggs to lend a different kind of richness. The method used here for poaching eggs will definitely test your patience, but it is a gentle method that lends itself to beautiful presentation and will protect the egg from direct poaching in water.

Eggs and truffles are a time-honored pairing. Truffle gatherers in rural backwoods France used to store their finds along with their eggs in the cellar. They found that a prized nugget of this elusive fungus in a basket of eggs would infuse the whole lot with an unmistakably earthy perfume. A delicacy was born; cheap and easy to cook up, the truffle-penetrated eggs in a soft state were the beginnings of a French gastronomic tradition. Here, a light brushing of truffle oil on the plastic wrap used to house the delicate egg as it poaches sets off the natural match. And of course, the croutons fried in olive oil make a cameo appearance to lend the crunch that this soft and supple salad needs.

Smoked Sturgeon /
Poached Egg / Olive Oil Croutons / Red Wine Vinaigrette

SERVES: 8

DIFFICULTY: Medium

Truffle oil, for brushing	
Salt and cracked black pepper to taste	
Organic eggs	8
Dijon mustard	1 tablespoon
Diced shallots	2
Red wine vinegar	¼ cup
Juice of ½ lemon	
Extra-virgin olive oil	1½ cups
Yellow baby frisée	2 heads, torn into small pieces
Flat-leaf parsley	½ bunch, leaves only
Shallots	2, thinly sliced
Olive-Oil-Fried Croutons (page 59)	
Smoked sturgeon	8 slices

Bring a medium pot of water to a boil.

To prepare the eggs, cut eight 5-inch pieces of butcher's twine. Line 8 coffee cups with plastic wrap, leaving 3 inches of overhanging wrap. Lightly but thoroughly brush the inside of the plastic wrap in each cup with the truffle oil, sprinkle with salt, and give it a turn of the pepper mill. Carefully crack each egg and pour into its own cup. Gather the plastic wrap from the back of the cup and gently pull forward in an upward motion, then down directly over the egg, sealing it in the wrap. Pull the egg in the wrap from the cup, then gather the plastic with your fingers at the top of the egg, to remove excess air. Carefully twist the wrap, allowing the air to escape. You are looking for a snug seal around the egg. Using the butcher's twine, tie the plastic right where it meets the egg, not allowing any slack. Cut the plastic

recipe continues...

wrap about 1 inch from the twine, and set the wrapped eggs aside in the refrigerator.

For the vinaigrette, using a small mixing bowl, whisk together the mustard, diced shallots, red wine vinegar, and lemon juice. Slowly drizzle in the olive oil while stirring constantly. Adjust the seasoning with salt and pepper.

Gently place the prepared eggs directly in the boiling water. Once the water has returned to a boil, reduce the heat to medium and cook for 4 minutes. Carefully remove the eggs from the water, and set aside.

To plate the salad, toss the frisée, parsley, thinly sliced shallots, and olive-oil-fried croutons with the vinaigrette. Line each salad bowl with a slice of smoked sturgeon. Arrange a small bed of the salad in the center. Place an egg on a kitchen spoon and, using scissors, cut the butcher's twine. Carefully remove the plastic wrap from the egg, and place the poached egg atop the greens. Serve immediately.

There is indeed such a thing as a chicken nugget for adults, and it's a chicken oyster. Practically at the backbone of the chicken between the thigh and rib cage, you'll find that decadent, delicious little oyster. You must pre-order these from the butcher as there are only two per bird. These lovelies stand up to hearty home-style cooking. And when they're incorporated into a pseudo-traditional variation of Italian piccata—smothering the sautéed pieces in juicy pan drippings, herbs, and a hit of lemon—it's a satisfying comfort meal for Sunday dinner.

For dredging, it's easier to prepare the chicken oysters Shake 'N Bake–style. Throw some flour in a resealable plastic bag, toss in the oysters, and shake it like you mean it.

Braised Chicken Oysters Piccata

SERVES: 8

DIFFICULTY: Medium

Chicken oysters	1 pound, picked through for bone fragments
All-purpose flour	2 tablespoons
Extra-virgin olive oil	¼ cup plus 1 tablespoon
Onion	½, diced
Garlic	5 medium cloves, sliced
White wine	½ cup (preferably pinot grigio)
Flat-leaf parsley	4 sprigs
Bay leaves	2
Thyme	2 sprigs
Chicken stock	2 cups
Juice of ½ lemon	
Unsalted butter	1 tablespoon, chilled
Chopped capers	1 teaspoon
Chopped flat-leaf parsley	1 tablespoon
Salt and cracked black pepper to taste	
Crusty bread	16 ½-inch-thick slices seasoned with the Garlic Love Rub (see page 52)

ALTERN8: Though we favor a braised preparation here since it's easier to control, you can make a "true" piccata by pounding out the oysters as we do at the restaurant à la minute.

Toss the chicken oysters with the flour in a medium resealable bag, and simply sieve to remove the excess flour.

Line a plate with a few paper towels, and set aside.

Heat a large sauté pan over medium-high heat, and add the ¼ cup of olive oil. Place all the chicken oysters in a single layer in the pan. Sauté until golden. Adjust the heat as needed; you want the pan to be hot enough to sauté the meat but not hot enough to burn the flour. Refrain from trying to flip the chicken in the pan, just cook thoroughly until crisp and golden on the first side for 3 minutes, turn individually, and cook the other side for 1 minute.

Once the nuggets are browned on both sides, slide them onto the prepared plate. Once the cooking oil is absorbed, discard the paper towels and allow the chicken juices to gather on the plate. Reserve.

Wipe out the oil from the sauté pan and return it to the heat. Add the remaining tablespoon of olive oil and the onion, and cook together for 2 minutes, stirring constantly. When the onion is

recipe continues...

recipe continued...

cooked and lightly caramelized, add the garlic and cook for 1 minute. Deglaze the pan with the white wine. Add the parsley, bay leaves, and thyme, then reduce until all the wine has evaporated, about 2 minutes.

Pour the chicken stock into the pan, and bring to a boil. Add the chicken nuggets and the natural juices that remain on the plate back into the pan. Bring to a boil, place a lid on the pan, then reduce the heat to low.

After the chicken has been simmering for 25 to 30 minutes, remove the lid and discard the herbs. Turn off the heat and allow the chicken to rest in its juices for 10 minutes.

When ready to serve, add the lemon juice and stir in the butter until it is all incorporated. This will thicken and enrich the sauce. In true piccata style, finish the sauce with the capers and chopped parsley, and season with salt and pepper. Serve with the toasted bread.

It's a bit of a holy triumvirate, the distinct combination of risotto, Parmesan, and orange-gold threads of saffron. Perhaps *the* official dish of Lombardy, Italy, risotto Milanese can also incorporate marrow to enrich this first-course wonder. If you pair it with an osso buco, you're in keeping with the traditions of braising shanks, though I like to use lamb instead of veal in this preparation, which you can precook two days ahead. To accommodate the small plate lounge diner, I use a 2-inch cut of lamb shank—perfect for just a few delicious bites of the rich, warm lamb.

Lamb Osso Buco /
Saffron Risotto Milanese

SERVES: 8

DIFFICULTY: Medium

LAMB OSSO BUCO

Lamb shank	8 medium pieces, 2-inch butcher's cut
Salt and cracked black pepper to taste	
Extra-virgin olive oil	1 tablespoon plus 1 teaspoon
Large-diced onion	½ cup
Diced celery	½ cup
Diced carrot	½ cup
Garlic	5 medium cloves, smashed
Red wine (cabernet sauvignon)	½ cup
Bouquet Garni (page 47)	
Lamb or beef broth	1¾ cups

SAFFRON RISOTTO MILANESE

Chicken stock or water	3 cups
Extra-virgin olive oil	2 tablespoons
Carnaroli rice	1 cup
Finely diced onion	2 tablespoons
Garlic	1 medium clove
Thyme	1 sprig
Bay leaf	1
White wine (preferably pinot grigio)	¼ cup
Saffron threads	¼ teaspoon, loosely packed
Salt	
Unsalted butter	2 tablespoons
Finely grated Parmesan cheese	½ cup
Cracked black pepper	

ALTERN8: Garnish this dish with Salsa Verde (page 29) and Toasted Bread Crumbs (page 43).

Save leftovers to make Wild Mushroom Risotto Balls (page 225).

Preheat the oven to 300°F.

For the osso buco, begin by heating a medium braising pan over medium-high heat. Season the lamb shanks with salt and pepper. Add 1 tablespoon of oil to the pan, and begin to sear the shanks on all sides until evenly browned, about 10 minutes. Remove the shanks from the pan and set aside on a plate. Wipe out and discard the oil, then return the pan to the heat.

Add the 1 teaspoon of olive oil to the pan over medium-high heat, and begin to caramelize the onion, celery, carrot, and garlic for approximately 6 to 8 minutes. Deglaze the pan with the wine, add the bouquet garni, and reduce the wine until dry, about 2 minutes. Place the shanks in the pan, wider side down, and pour the broth over them. (The broth should cover just the lower half of the shanks.) Bring the braise to a boil, cover, and place in the oven for 1 hour. Turn the shanks over, skim the fat, cover, and braise for another 30 minutes. Remove the lid, skim again, and baste the shanks with the braising juice every 10 minutes until cooked, about 30 to 45 minutes. The meat should be very tender and easily removed from the bone.

Once the meat is fully cooked, allow the shanks to cool in their own juices at room temperature. As they cool, try to skim and discard as much as possible of the fat that will rise to the top. Once the shanks are cooled and well rested, remove them and strain the juice. Place the juice back onto the stove over medium-high heat, and warm through for 10 minutes, reducing the liquid by half and

recipe continues...

Educ8: Risotto Rapture

Risotto is one of the creamiest, sexiest dishes out there. To do it right, give it the time and attention it needs to release its natural starches. If you're serving a stirred risotto (using only a wooden spoon), keep it on the al dente side. That texture and creaminess come from the slow, simmered stirring of the whole grains of rice, not from the butter and cheese (they enhance the flavor after the fact). Use Arborio, Carnaroli, or, for accompanying quail or small game, small-grain Vialone Nano.

Short on time? Precook the risotto most of the way and cool long before your guests arrive; otherwise, it can take more than a full half hour from start to finish. When it's time to eat, reheat, season, finish with the butter and cheese, and serve. (Some hard-core Italian chefs might put a hit out on me for saying this; they'll only serve risotto cooked without interruption from raw to finished.)

Remember that the addition of saffron is just about perfuming the rice, not going for color (that's what I like to call expensive overkill). It should be a subtle hint that doesn't fight the simple, clean flavor of the toothsome rice; it should keep you wanting more.

recipe continued...

skimming to clarify. Rest the shanks back in the liquid. Set aside for 30 minutes and keep warm while cooking the risotto.

To prepare the saffron risotto, bring the stock to a boil in a small sauce pot and set aside. In a medium, heavy-bottomed stockpot over medium-high heat, add the olive oil. Add the Carnaroli rice and begin to stir the rice with a wooden spoon, coating and heating it in the oil—but not forming any color. Once the rice is completely warm to the touch but not toasted or colored, add the onion, garlic clove, thyme, and bay leaf, stirring constantly. Cook the vegetables until translucent, stirring all the while, about 5 minutes. Deglaze the pan with the white wine, add the saffron, and reduce for 30 seconds or until dry. Begin adding the stock $\frac{1}{4}$ cup at a time while stirring, and add the next $\frac{1}{4}$ cup only after the preceding has been fully absorbed. During this process, after 10 minutes, reduce the heat to medium; after the following 10 minutes, add a pinch of salt. Continue to cook and add the stock until the rice is perfectly al dente, for a total cooking time of about 25 minutes. Remove from the heat and stir in the butter and Parmesan cheese, then season with salt and pepper.

Spoon into 8 bowls and place 1 shank on top of each. Pour a little of the braising juice directly on the shank, and serve.

I had a late-night craving for something warm and fuzzy, and I had some leftover new potatoes wrapped up in the fridge. I pulled them out, heated them through in the oven, then topped the spuds with some double-crème Brie and tossed a few leaves of emerald-green arugula on the side. I had eaten most of my pickled red onions as the cheese melted in the broiler, but I managed to save a few for a garnish. What a snack.

When you want to curl up on a chilly day in front of the fire, this shortcut to a Swiss raclette really does the trick. Whereas you scrape that mellow and nutty cow's-milk cheese as it melts off a hot stone in the open fire, here, it's easiest to melt some Brie and broil it until crusty and gooey.

Warm New Potatoes /
Melted Brie / Baby Arugula

SERVES: 8

DIFFICULTY: Easy

New potatoes	16
Salt	
Canola oil	2 tablespoons
Brie	¼ pound
Cracked black pepper	
Baby arugula, for garnish	
Pickled Red Onions (page 35), for garnish	

Boil the new potatoes in salted water until fully cooked, about 10 to 15 minutes.

Preheat the broiler.

Peel the potatoes and place the skins in a small pot with the canola oil. Bring the oil up to medium heat and cook the skins until crisp.

On a small baking sheet, "crack" the potatoes in half with a fork. Stick under the broiler until lightly roasted. Top the potatoes with slices of Brie (rind on) and place back under the broiler just long enough to melt the cheese.

Divide the potatoes onto small plates and season them with salt and pepper. Sprinkle the arugula and crisped skins on top as garnish, and serve immediately with the pickled red onions as a condiment on the side.

For a couple months at a time, we're lucky enough to source young and beautiful baby broccoli. The mildness of this labor-intensive seasonal vegetable is faintly reminiscent of asparagus, and you can eat the tender stalks and florets in one bite. Not to be confused with bitter broccoli rabe, its sweet flavor gets really concentrated with pan roasting. The gentle drizzle of the *bagna cauda*–esque warm anchovy vinaigrette imparts a lush and buttery, briny element to the dish. On our lounge menu, we either serve this preparation or we gratinée them with an herbed hollandaise and plenty of freshly grated Parmesan cheese.

Charred Baby Broccoli /
Marinated Peppers / Warm Anchovy Vinaigrette

SERVES: 8

DIFFICULTY: Easy

Unsalted butter	5 tablespoons
Chopped garlic	1 medium clove
Long zest of ½ lemon, sliced thin lengthwise	
White anchovy	1 ounce, cut into thirds
Extra-virgin olive oil	⅛ cup plus 2 tablespoons
Juice of 1 lemon	
Salt and pepper to taste	
Baby broccoli	2 pounds
Marinated Roasted Peppers (page 34)	½ cup, about 3 medium

ALTERN8: Sprinkle with Toasted Bread Crumbs (page 43).

You can use regular anchovies in a pinch.

You may use either broccolini or broccoli rabe if no baby broccoli is available.

For the warm anchovy vinaigrette, in a small saucepan over low heat, melt 3 tablespoons of the butter with the chopped garlic. Add the lemon zest, anchovy, and ⅛ cup of olive oil. Simmer for 5 minutes and adjust the seasoning with the lemon juice, salt, and pepper. Set aside and keep warm while cooking the baby broccoli.

Working in 2 batches, in a cast-iron pan over medium-high heat, add 1 tablespoon of the olive oil. Place half of the broccoli in the pan, spreading it out in a single layer over the base of the entire pan. Add 1 tablespoon of the butter and dot it throughout. Try not to move the broccoli too much — this is how you obtain that wonderful char. Leave it to cook for 2½ minutes on each side. Turn the heat off and allow the broccoli to rest for 5 minutes. Season with salt and pepper. Set aside, then repeat this process with the remaining broccoli, olive oil, and butter.

To serve, place the charred broccoli in a small serving dish. Toss with the marinated peppers and drizzle with the warm anchovy vinaigrette. Feel free to finish the dish with toasted bread crumbs if you've got 'em.

The natural sweetness of the carrot can be taken all the way home in an indulgent, comforting carrot cake. We like to load up the dessert menu at Table 8 with reinterpretations of home-style desserts that are still sophisticated enough to not abandon French technique.

Here, a classic cream-cheese frosting goes for broke as a mousse. Instead of the super-airy, fluffy mousse of egg whites to which you might be accustomed, this decadent cream cheese mousse uses the foundation of a pâte à bombe. This is a pâtisserie-style process whereby egg yolks are whipped into sugar syrup that's been cooked to (in this case) hard-ball consistency, then aerated until light and increased in volume. To do this, you fold in a combination of sugar, gelatin, whipped cream, and flavoring (here, old-school cream cheese). The pâte à bombe works well as a base for buttercreams and parfaits, too.

The citrus reduction, "adult Fruit Roll-Up" carrot leather, and candied pecans are easy to make and are complementary garnishes, though they're optional if you're short on time. Remember, the devil is in the details, and these little extras really complete this dish.

Carrot Cake /
Cream Cheese Mousse

SERVES: 8

DIFFICULTY: Challenging

CARROT CAKE

Eggs	4
Vegetable oil	1½ cups
Vanilla extract	2 tablespoons
Grated carrots	2½ cups
Granulated sugar	1½ cups
Brown sugar	½ cup
Ground cinnamon	1 tablespoon
All-purpose flour	2 cups
Baking soda	1½ teaspoons
Salt	½ teaspoon

CREAM CHEESE MOUSSE

Heavy cream	2½ cups
Confectioners' sugar	3 tablespoons
Egg yolks	5
Granulated sugar	⅔ cup
Powdered gelatin	2 tablespoons
Cream cheese	16 ounces, room temperature

CARROT LEATHER

Carrots	3 medium
Juice of ½ lemon	
Sugar	1 cup
Pectin	⅔ cup

CITRUS REDUCTION

Sugar	1½ cups
Lemon juice	3 tablespoons
Orange juice	2 cups
Zest of 1 orange	
Apricot jelly	¼ cup

CANDIED PECANS

Sugar	2 cups
Whole pecans	1 cup

Preheat the oven to 350°F.

For the carrot cake, mix the eggs, oil, and vanilla extract together in a large bowl. Add the grated carrots. Sift the dry ingredients together in a separate small bowl, and combine into the wet mixture. Spray a 9 x 14-inch rimmed sheet pan with nonstick baking spray, pour the batter into the pan, and bake for 25 to 30 minutes, or until the center springs back to the touch like it would with a pound cake. Cool the cake in the pan for 15 minutes, then transfer to a rack to cool completely.

For the cream cheese mousse, in an electric mixer, whip the heavy cream with the confectioners' sugar to medium-stiff peaks until well incorporated. Set aside. In a clean bowl, whip the egg yolks until they're pale and fluffy and doubled in volume.

While the egg yolks are beating, in a small sauce pot over medium heat, cook the sugar and 3 tablespoons water to hard-ball consistency (using a candy thermometer to 120°C or 248°F). Using a brush, make sure the sides of the pan are free from sugar crystals by brushing down with water. Slowly pour the cooked sugar into the whipped egg yolks, still mixing at high speed with an electric mixer until cooled. While this is mixing, bloom the gelatin as instructed on the package, discarding the liquid.

In a large bowl, pour the bloomed gelatin into the cream cheese and using a whisk, incorporate thoroughly. Combine the egg and sugar mixture into the cream cheese, and mix well. Fold in the whipped cream, then place in the fridge to set up.

recipe continues...

For the carrot leather, boil the carrots for 8 to 10 minutes in water to cover. Drain, leaving just a bit of the cooking liquid to aid in blending. Using a food processor, purée the carrots until still chunky but fairly smooth. In a small sauce pot over medium heat, combine the carrots, the lemon juice, and half the sugar, and bring to a boil. Mix the pectin with the remaining ½ cup of sugar and add to the mixture, boiling for 1½ to 2 minutes and stirring constantly so the pectin doesn't clump. Remove from the heat, and spread onto a dry Silpat or silicone mat (it's easier to handle if it's spread a bit thicker). Allow to cool in the fridge.

For the citrus reduction, combine all ingredients in a small saucepan over medium-low heat. Watching so that the mixture doesn't boil over, reduce to a saucelike consistency so that it coats a spoon, about 10 minutes. Keep warm.

Finally, for the candied pecans, begin by preheating the oven to 350°F.

Bring the sugar and 2 cups water to a boil in a sauce pot. Add the pecans and cook for 10 to 15 minutes. Drain well. Transfer the mixture to a sheet pan and bake until caramelized with a medium-deep color, about 25 minutes.

To plate this dish, cut the fruit leather out into desired shapes once set. Spoon the cream cheese mousse onto the cake, smoothly spread with an offset steel spatula, and allow to set in the refrigerator for at least 30 minutes before cutting. Using a knife with a thin blade, dip the blade into hot water and cut the cake into 2-inch squares, keeping the blade clean for each cut. (Prepare to end up with some leftovers for snacking.) For each serving, drizzle the citrus reduction around the plate, and sprinkle with the candied pecans. Lay the carrot leather on top as a garnish.

My friend Chris, a seasoned bar manager here in Los Angeles, got this recipe from his uncle Al in Philadelphia. A seasonal egg-free holiday drink that's really light and boozy (as opposed to dense and cloying spiked eggnog), this is the kind of satisfying drink that doesn't induce nausea past the first eight ounces. A little Southern Comfort and a zesty sprig of rosemary will go a long way to bring in the cheer. If you're lucky, you'll be "noggin' it" all night long.

Noggin' It

MAKES: 1 gallon

DIFFICULTY: Easy

Southern Comfort	12 ounces
Light rum	6 ounces
Brandy	6 ounces
Vodka	3 ounces
Whole milk	8 ounces
Ground nutmeg to taste	
Superfine sugar, for garnish (optional)	
Rosemary sprigs, for garnish	

In a large pitcher, stir together the Southern Comfort, rum, brandy, vodka, and milk. Season with the nutmeg. Serve either shaken in a martini glass rimmed with superfine sugar, or in a rocks glass over ice. Garnish each glass with a rosemary sprig.

On the occasional late night in the lounge, Andrew would play barkeep and make some very funky concoctions. I'm sure the alcoholic take on the creamsicle has been done before, but here, tangerines, not oranges, make a vibrant punch. It's no secret that California is citrus country (watch out, Florida!). If you spot me in the kitchen in the early winter, chances are I'm peeling one of these little tangerine gems. Some of my favorite varieties come from nearby groves like Tom's, Perfection, and the well-known Pixie from Ojai. Add a touch of vanilla and some cream to this cocktail, and it'll take you straight back to summers at the pool with the jingle-jangle of the ice cream truck ringing in the distance.

Table 8 Creamsicle

SERVES: 1

DIFFICULTY: Easy

Peeled tangerine	1
Granulated sugar	2 teaspoons
Stoli Vanil vodka	4 ounces
Juice of 3 tangerines	
Half-and-half	1 tablespoon
Superfine sugar, for garnish	

ALTERN8: The trusty clementine has earned a soft spot in my heart and can easily stand in for the tangerine.

In a tumbler, lightly muddle the tangerine with the granulated sugar. Add the vodka, tangerine juice, and half-and-half. Transfer to a cocktail shaker filled with ice. Rim the tumbler with superfine sugar, and strain the creamsicle into the glass and serve.

While you and your guests are perched on the couch with the football game blaring during Thanksgiving, the steady flow of beer can become a little too much for daytime. This nonalcoholic mocktail is not syrupy like the canned variety, but there's plenty of diced fruit to munch on while you imbibe.

To make your own cranberry juice, take whole pots almost full of washed cranberries, cover them with water, add sugar to taste in order to mellow the cran's tartness, and simply cook them until they are soft. (And if you really want to doctor this up, a little bourbon from Uncle Bob's monogrammed hip flask will get the party started.)

Cranberry Fruit Cocktail

SERVES: 8

DIFFICULTY: Easy

White cranberry juice	4 cups
Cranberry juice	4 cups
Orange juice	2 cups
Grapes	1 pint, split in half lengthwise
Oranges	6, peeled and cut into segments
Limes	2, peeled and cut into segments
Medium-size apples	2, peeled and cut into large dice

In a large bowl or pitcher, combine the cranberry juices with the orange juice. Add the grapes, oranges, limes, and apples, and chill. Serve in a cold punch bowl or pitcher.

With global warming and an already fabulous subtropical climate, summers never seem to end in Los Angeles. A backdrop of fizzy champagne makes this combination of late-summer fruit—honeydew, strawberry, and peach—sparkle with festival splendor. Feel free to use any light and crisp bubbly, from Italian prosecco to Spanish cava, California sparkling to French champagne.

Indian Summer Punch

SERVES: 8

DIFFICULTY: Easy

Sugar	½ cup
Honeydew juice	4 cups
Strawberry juice	1 cup
Peach nectar	2 cups
Lemon juice	1 cup
Champagne	2 bottles, chilled
Mint	½ bunch, for garnish

ALTERN8: If you cannot find honeydew juice, any melon juice will do.

To make your own melon juice, simply purée fresh melon in a blender with just enough water to liquefy, and strain.

In a large pitcher, dissolve the sugar in the honeydew, strawberry, peach, and lemon juice. Chill. Just before serving, pour the juice mixture into a cold punch bowl and top with the champagne. Garnish with mint sprigs.

d8

sexy savories

Tangerine Scream

Truffled Gruyère Fondue

Kumamoto Oysters / American Caviar / Champagne Granita

Tuna Tartare Niçoise

Heart & Sole

Buckwheat Crepes / Blood Orange / Gelato

Breakfast in Bed

Passion Fruit Bellini

D8 Strawberry Lassi

Table 8 Bloody Mary

The Dirty Virgin

Whether you're wandering

through the farmer's markets with a loved one on a sensual Saturday, preparing a romantic dinner for two, or eating breakfast in bed on a lazy Sunday, food can be sexy. The trick is setting the right tone—candles, flowers, garnishes—paired with the right flavors and textures. If you're entertaining a new friend, the truffled Gruyère fondue is playful, interactive, even flirtatious; if you're going straight for romance, try the oysters with a champagne granita as an aphrodisiac. When cooking for someone special, it doesn't make sense to spend all of your time in the kitchen once he or she has arrived. Make sure to prep ahead and have those tangerine screams ready so they're in hand as soon as you've opened the door.

Tangerine Scream

SERVES: 1	
DIFFICULTY: Easy	

Juice of 3 medium tangerines

| Rum | 2 ounces |
| Triple Sec | ½ ounce |

Splash of sweet-and-sour mix

Tangerine segments, for garnish

ALTERN8: **No tangerines in sight? Two small oranges will suffice.**

Pour the tangerine juice, rum, Triple Sec, and sweet-and-sour mix into a cocktail shaker. Strain into a tumbler with crushed ice. Garnish with skewered tangerine segments.

This especially intense

version of an orange juice–rum Shark Bite takes advantage of seasonal tangerines and their vivid color. In the winter, when temperatures drop and the days are short, this sun-soaked cocktail will whisk you away to a rooftop party at the Regent South Beach.

When we opened Table 8, this was one of the first dishes to find its way onto the lounge menu—and it's remained ever since. A perennial favorite, fondue is the quintessential lounge food because it's perfect for sharing. After dipping the crusty sourdough cubes into aromatic truffled cheese, skip the forks and feed each other with your fingers. While each cook has his or her own preference for a fondue cheese mix, I like to go for something not too overpowering, like a good-quality alpine Gruyère and a cave-aged Emmentaler. Together, the two cheeses have excellent "string" factor; when you can stretch out the melted cheese to arm's length and it's still attached to the fondue pot, it's a good sign. Of course, adding that small amount of earthy truffle oil makes a simple dish even more impressive.

Truffled Gruyère Fondue

SERVES: 2

DIFFICULTY: Easy

White wine (preferably a riesling)	¼ cup
Minced garlic	½ teaspoon
Truffled cheese	1 ounce, shredded
Gruyère cheese	1 ounce, shredded
Pinch of cornstarch	
Salt to taste	
Lightly toasted sourdough boule, crusts removed, and sliced into 1-inch cubes	

ALTERN8: Try asparagus and cauliflower or pears and apples on the side as additional dipping vehicles.

If you can't find truffled cheese, substitute Emmentaler and add in ½ teaspoon of white or black truffle oil.

In a small saucepan over high heat, add the wine and the garlic. Once the wine boils, lower the heat to medium. Reduce the wine to cook off the alcohol, approximately 2 minutes, then add the cheeses and stir constantly with a wooden spoon. Add the cornstarch, and continue to stir until melted and smooth but not runny, about 4 to 5 minutes. Add more wine if it's too tight. Season with salt, pour into a warmed fondue pot, and serve with the bread cubes.

Those who like to go down that truly traditional aphrodisiac road will appreciate this application of champagne with these treasures of the sea. I served this on a Valentine's Day menu once, and it was a hit with couples who loved the sensual combination of caviar and champagne with slippery oysters. Best of all, the twist: The icy crunch of a bubbly-based granita lends cool textural interest to this easy appetizer.

While osetra from the Caspian Sea stands out as a connoisseur's favorite, I prefer American caviar because it's sustainable. The farms raising these fish use all parts of the sturgeon and paddlefish instead of discarding them once the precious roe has been extracted from the belly.

Kumamoto Oysters /
American Caviar / Champagne Granita

SERVES: 2

DIFFICULTY: Easy

Champagne	½ cup
Champagne vinegar	1 tablespoon
Salt	
Kumamoto oysters	1 dozen, shucked
American caviar	1 ounce
Diced chives, for garnish	1 tablespoon
Diced shallot, for garnish	1 tablespoon
Chopped flat-leaf parsley, for garnish	1 tablespoon
Freshly cracked black pepper	

In a small bowl, stir together the bubbly and the champagne vinegar with 2 tablespoons water, and freeze for 1 hour. Once the granita is frozen solid, use a fork to scrape the ice into fine shavings, and place in another chilled bowl. Store in the freezer until the last second before serving.

In a small serving bowl, place a wad of folded paper towels on the bottom to absorb any water from the melting ice. Place freshly crushed ice in the bowl, and sprinkle with a pinch of salt (this will keep the ice colder and solid). Place a ramekin in the center of the ice, and arrange 6 of the oysters around it. Add a nice dollop of caviar on top of each oyster. I like to serve 6 at a time, so keep the others in the fridge, ready for the second wave. Toss the chopped herbs and shallot into the bowl of shaved granita and mix thoroughly. Season with a few turns of the pepper mill; place the granita in the ramekin. If you really want to go romantic, sneak in some rose petals on top of the ice. Don't be afraid to feed each other!

Educ8: Oyster Cult

When working with shellfish, you want to keep all your ingredients as cold as possible and fresh down to the last second. Shucking oysters way ahead of time is a first-class ticket to an unappetizingly desiccated fruit of the sea.

As far as most shellfish is concerned, I subscribe to the adage that you only purchase oysters in months that end with an "R." I am not a huge fan of oysters in general, but if I must, the only oyster I eat is the Kumamoto; it's small in size with sweet meat and less of the metallicy briny taste often associated with a plumper variety. And whether you want to call it jus, nectar, or liquor, the best part of the oyster is that delicious liquid inside. When shucking, reserve as much as you can in the shell.

As for any seafood, it's important to purchase oysters from a reputable source. Ask your fishmonger what date the oysters were harvested; if he or she has no idea, that's a tip to make a beeline out of there. At the restaurant, we never use any oyster that's five days past harvest date. Be as complusive as you can about this; you'll be thankful that you were.

Bad oysters can be found in even the best dozen from the most expensive purveyor. There are plenty of cues to the occasional one that's "off." The best rule, though, is common sense. If you open it and it looks dry or shriveled or doesn't smell like a fresh ocean breeze, don't even question it. Throw it away.

As for the proper shucking technique, here's a situation where the right tool is paramount. Use an oyster knife and only an oyster knife. (Otherwise, you're guaranteed a date in the emergency room.) First, rinse the oyster well in cold running water. Cupping it in your hand, place the oyster with the eye facing toward you. Using a kitchen towel and a steady hand, firmly and carefully pierce the eye with the tip of the oyster knife. Straighten out the blade, and draw it straight back to release the muscle holding the shell together. Discard the top shell. Be careful to look for any dangerous and unpleasant shards of oyster shell. Using the oyster knife, scoop under the oyster meat to release it from the underside of the shell.

Here's a refreshing alternative to the classic southern Provençal salad that's seemingly a lunchtime staple in California restaurants. All the basics are in there in one guise or another, from tuna and hard-boiled egg to haricots verts and deep, rich olives. Here, raw sushi-grade tuna and a tiny quail egg accompany a small bunch of blanched beans with an overall drizzle of olivey tapenade vinaigrette. This sexy rendition is easily prepared in advance and quickly assembled. You can make the chips ahead of time, just be sure to store them in a warm dry spot and try not to eat them all!

Tuna Tartare Niçoise

SERVES: 2	
DIFFICULTY: Easy	

Sushi-grade tuna	4 ounces, cut into small dice
Canola oil, for frying	
Kennebec or Russet potatoes	2 small
Sea salt and cracked black pepper to taste	
Chives	6
French green beans (haricots verts)	3 ounces, blanched
Extra-virgin olive oil	2 tablespoons
Tapenade (page 31) or chopped olives	1 tablespoon
Juice of ½ lemon	
Quail egg	1, hard-boiled for 5 minutes, peeled, cut in half
Marinated Roasted Peppers (page 34)	

Gently place the diced tuna into 2 chilled ring molds onto 2 small plates. Cover with plastic wrap and refrigerate.

Heat 2 inches of canola oil in a medium sauce pot to 350°F.

Thinly slice the potatoes on a mandoline. Fry in the oil until crisp and golden. Drain well on paper towels, and season with salt and pepper.

Lay 3 chives vertically on a smooth surface, and place half of the beans on top, perpendicular to the chives. Tie knots around the beans using the chives. You want the beans cut to equal length. Leave the nice tips and cut the bottoms. Repeat with the remaining chives and beans.

Whisk 1 tablespoon of the olive oil into the tapenade. Set aside.

Remove the ring molds and season the tuna with a small amount of salt and pepper, a squeeze of lemon juice, and 1 tablespoon olive oil. Lay the green beans to the side of the tuna, and place a small stack of the potato chips in between. Garnish the top of each portion of the tuna with the halved quail egg, and drizzle each plate with the tapenade. Scatter a few of the marinated peppers on each plate and serve.

Educ8: Prepping a Fish

If your seafood monger forgets to prepare your fish, here's the shortcut way to remove the skin and head. Taking a pair of kitchen shears, cut close around the fins and cut the head off. Next, dip *only* the tail of the fish in boiling water and lay it flat on a dry cutting board. Using a towel, quickly and simply rub the skin from the tip of the tailbone toward the head until there is enough skin to get a good grip. Carefully pull the skin upward and toward the head while holding the tail firmly in place with the other hand. Flip the fish over and remove the skin from the other side, and voilà! You're good to go.

As far as I'm concerned, sole is the king of fish and a perfect dish for two. One sole feeds a couple, and the flesh is ideally balanced: mild in flavor and firm in texture. Truth be told, it's pretty much guaranteed to seal the deal if you serve this to your date.

Unless you're a master at filleting anything tableside, retreat to the kitchen and prepare this simple dish. Go ahead and present the whole cooked fish to your date, then run back while it's still hot. Filleting a sole may sound daunting, but by using a spatula, it can be done easily.

Heart & Sole

SERVES: 2

DIFFICULTY: Easy

Chinese long beans	6 strands (approximately 2½ ounces)
Dover sole	1 16- to 20-ounce fillet, skin off, bone in, and head removed
Salt and pepper to taste	
All-purpose flour	½ cup
Grapeseed or canola oil	2 tablespoons
Unsalted butter	4 tablespoons (½ stick)
Diced shallot	1 tablespoon
Chopped flat-leaf parsley	1 tablespoon
Dry white wine	3 tablespoons
Juice of ½ lemon	

ALTERN8: If you're not up for the Dover sole challenge just yet, try experimenting with sand dabs. Locally caught in California, they're somewhat of a distant cousin but still in the sole family. They're less expensive and can be filleted in the same way. While you're trying to master the fillet routine, practice in the kitchen a few times on some sand dabs before moving up to the dining room with the elegant (and pricey) Dover sole!

To get the long beans ready, simply blanch them in boiling water for 3 minutes. Shock them in an ice-water bath for a minute or until they are cooled. Grab 3 strands and cut off the tips. Then, tying with butcher's twine or kitchen string at one end to secure, braid the strands together. You will need one braid for each plate.

Preheat the oven to 350°F.

Season the sole liberally with salt and pepper. Dredge it in just enough flour to coat, then pat off the excess.

Using an ovenproof large sauté pan over medium-high heat, add the grapeseed oil. Add the fish, and allow it to cook for 1 minute. Add 1 tablespoon of the butter and allow it to cook for another minute. Flip the fish, cook for an additional minute, then place in the oven to cook for 4 minutes. The fish will be cooked perfectly when the flesh just starts to pull from the spine. Using a spatula, pull the fish out of the pan and rest it on a plate (you'll be collecting the jus from the fish).

recipe continues...

To fillet the sole, transfer to a cutting board. With a large spoon, scrape away the pin bones and discard. If it's cooked through, the bones should pull away very easily. Place a plastic spatula right under the meat at the head of the fish. Holding the fish steady, slide the spatula straight back to remove it from the spine, keeping the spatula resting directly on the bone and on a slight angle to shovel the spatula under the flesh. Keep the fish right where it is and repeat this process on the underside (right on top of the meat below the spine with the spatula at a slight pitch up toward the bone).

Over medium heat, add the diced shallot to the same sauté pan and sauté until translucent. Add the parsley and white wine. Turn the heat off, add 1 tablespoon of water, and whisk in the remaining 3 tablespoons of butter until thoroughly melted. Season with salt and pepper and the lemon juice and pour the fish jus back into the pan. Add the braided beans to warm through (without the heat), and serve immediately with the fish. For a fancy (though inedible) garnish, scrub and rinse the spine. Gently bend the bone into a circle, tie with butcher's twine, and deep-fry until crisp and golden.

Crepes are my easy out. Great as a standby, they can be made well ahead of time and even frozen, so you can always have a few on hand to pull out of the freezer in the event of a hospitality emergency. In fact, every component in this dish can be prepared in advance and swapped out to your liking. Use figs instead of blood oranges; use strawberries instead of figs; interchange the gelato flavors . . . be seasonal and get creative.

Buckwheat Crepes /
Blood Orange / Gelato

SERVES: 2

DIFFICULTY: Easy

Unsalted butter	2 tablespoons
Buckwheat flour	⅓ cup plus 1 tablespoon
All-purpose flour	⅛ cup
Salt	¼ teaspoon
Egg yolk	1
Whole milk	½ cup
Granulated sugar	½ tablespoon
Armagnac	2 tablespoons
Blood oranges	1 zested and juiced; 2 whole, segmented
Gelato	2 scoops, preferably fig-Armagnac, or zabaglione
Confectioners' sugar, for dusting	

Melt 1 tablespoon of the butter in a small saucepan over low heat and set aside.

In a large bowl, sift together the flours and salt, and make a well in the center. Whisk the egg yolk into the center of the flour and mix thoroughly. Slowly add half the milk while gradually drawing in the flour with the whisk to make a smooth batter. Stir in the melted butter and the remaining milk. Allow this mixture to rest for 2 hours in the refrigerator.

In a small saucepan, melt the sugar in 1 table-spoon of water. Reduce this mixture by half, approximately 1 minute, then add the Armagnac and reduce by half again for another minute. Add the blood orange juice and reduce to a light, thin syrup, about 2 minutes. Add half of the blood orange zest (save the rest for another use) and cook together for 1 minute. Add the segments and heat through. Then keep warm.

After the batter has rested, check its consistency and ensure that it is like a thin cream. Melt the remaining tablespoon of butter in a small saucepan over low heat. Heat an 8-inch nonstick pan over medium heat. Brush with the melted butter. Pour a small amount of batter into the pan. Tilt and swirl the pan until the batter has thinly covered the bottom, then pour any remaining batter back into the bowl. Cook until lightly browned, then flip using a plastic spatula. The total cooking time for each crepe should be about 1 minute. Make the rest of the crepes now and freeze.

On each plate, fold a crepe into fourths, and place one scoop of the gelato on the crepe. Pour some of the blood orange mixture around the crepe, and dust with the confectioners' sugar.

Breakfast in bed is the secret weapon to impress. Could it get any more deluxe than a creamy asparagus and morel mushroom omelet, broiled up with melted Drunken Goat cheese? These tasty morsels can tip the indulgence scales so your Sunday in bed with *The New York Times* and a loved one is pure luxury. You can easily sneak to the kitchen without making too much noise for this ultimate surprise. If you've prepared the morels and asparagus and beaten the eggs the night before, then assembling the elegant omelet requires little effort.

Breakfast in Bed

SERVES: 2

DIFFICULTY: Easy

Morel mushrooms	4 medium-size
Jumbo asparagus	3
Eggs	4
Salt and pepper to taste	
Crème fraîche (or sour cream)	2 tablespoons
Grapeseed or canola oil	4 teaspoons
Unsalted butter, to coat the pan	
Drunken Goat cheese	4 thin slices

ALTERN8: If morels aren't in season, substitute shiitake mushrooms.

If Drunken Goat cheese isn't at hand, use any fresh or aged goat cheese.

You can place the cheese inside the omelet as well.

Clean the morels thoroughly, remove the stems, and then cut them into ¼-inch rings. For the asparagus, trim the ends, peel about 4 inches from the bottom of the stalk, and cut thinly on a bias.

Crack the eggs into a bowl and season them with salt and pepper. Whisk together, add the crème fraîche, and whisk together very well until smooth.

In a nonstick omelet pan or skillet over medium-high heat, add 2 teaspoons of the grapeseed oil. Sauté the mushrooms until fully cooked, about 2 minutes. Season with salt and pepper, and set aside. Repeat this process with the asparagus. You want a little bit of color to the vegetables, but you don't want to pan-roast them.

In an 8-inch omelet pan over medium-high heat, add just enough butter to coat the pan. Add half of the egg batter, and use a rubber spatula to spread it out (keeping a thick bed of egg on the bottom), patting down as it cooks. Remove from the heat and add half of the sautéed vegetables on half of the omelet. Very carefully, flip half of it over to form the traditional half-moon omelet and let the eggs "congeal" to your liking. Place 2 slices of cheese on top and broil until the cheese is just melted. Slide the omelet onto a plate and keep warm. Repeat with the remaining ingredients to form a second omelet. Serve immediately.

Passion Fruit Bellini

SERVES: 2

DIFFICULTY: Easy

Passion fruit purée (store-bought)	1 tablespoon
Passion fruit	1
Champagne, to pour	

Divide the purée into two champagne flutes. Scoop the flesh of the passion fruit on top of the purée, and slowly pour the champagne to fill each glass.

The Bellini brunch is so old-school that it's making a retro comeback. But after a while, that flute of peachy nectar and good bubbly can get a little tired. Why not go a bit more exotic with the hit of tart and acidic passion fruit for a sweet morning wake-up call?

It's always fascinating to look to historical food and drink as precursors to today's hippest culinary trends. While Californians popularized smoothies in the 1990s, Indians have been frothing up nutritious yogurt beverages since ancient times. For the lassi, a base of thick real yogurt (none of that fat-free Splenda-fied kind) combines with unctuous honey and a wide array of spices and herbs like dry-roasted cumin and chili, mint, and ginger. Sometimes blended up with buttermilk to make it like a rich milkshake, these drinks can be as airy and frothy or as dense as you desire. Historically, the salty lassi originated first, followed by sweet variations mixed with anything from fresh mango pulp to precious saffron. Here, I like to make a California-Indian connection with ingredients grown in both lands: plump Medjool dates and ripe strawberries.

D8 Strawberry Lassi

SERVES: 2

DIFFICULTY: Easy

Plain yogurt	1 pint
Whole milk	1 pint
Medjool dates	6, chopped into small pieces
Ripe strawberries	4
Juice of ½ lime	
Small pinch of salt	

Place the yogurt, milk, dates, strawberries, lime juice, and salt in a blender. Process until frothy and smooth.

In my estimation, there are at least 110 ways to make this spicy eye-opener; here's how it's served at Table 8. When in season, colorful local varieties of heirloom tomato make a great base for my classic version. A pinch of this, a dash of that, and the only other thing you need is a celery stick to stir around the Bloody Mary's veggie-packed boozy goodness.

Table 8 Bloody Mary

SERVES: 2

DIFFICULTY: Easy

Tomato juice	8 ounces
Vodka	4 ounces
Dash of Worcestershire sauce	
Dash of Tabasco sauce	
Juice of ½ lime	
Celery salt, for rim garnish	
Cracked black pepper to taste	
Fresh grated horseradish to taste	
Celery heart stalk, for garnish	

In a cocktail shaker with plenty of ice, shake the tomato juice, vodka, Worcestershire, Tabasco, and lime juice. Strain into two pint glasses rimmed with celery salt. Garnish with a few turns of the pepper mill and grated horseradish. Swizzle each glass with a celery heart stalk.

ALTERN8: Using the recipe for Pickled Red Onions (page 35), quick-pickle some asparagus or baby corn for something a little out of the ordinary. Or plop in a few tomolives (small pickled green tomatoes) from a gourmet shop.

Instead of tomato juice, try using the Wood-Roasted Gazpacho (page 95) for the best Bloody Mary ever!

The Dirty Virgin

SERVES: 1

DIFFICULTY: Easy

Jack Daniel's	2 ounces
Ginger ale	2 ounces
Cranberry juice	1 ounce
Lime wedge, for garnish	

Pour the whiskey, soda, and juice into a highball glass filled with ice, and garnish with a lime wedge.

This quaffable beverage

started out as a refreshing virgin cocktail. One day, it seemed to call out for a shot of whiskey, thus transforming into a "dirty" virgin. Add one ounce of your favorite Tennessee moonshine, and you and your date can toast the South.

18 night

lounge foods

Truffled Yukon Gold Potato Chips

Wild Mushroom Risotto Balls / Burrata / Scallion Oil

Fried Seppie / Fried Artichoke

Brandade Fritters / Wood-Roasted Tomato Coulis

Scotch Quail Eggs / Chorizo

Smashed Spuds / Sliced Beef / Blue Cheese

Grilled Cheese / Pulled Short Ribs / Pickled Red Onions

Grilled Pizzetta / Roasted Artichoke / Tomato / Red Hawk Cheese

Krispy Kreme "Coffee & Doughnuts"

Kona Coffee Kicker

Buena Vista Rum Punch

Guaro Goofy Juice

Prior to opening Table 8, we cleared out a few walls in one section of the restaurant. When looking at the raw space, we knew we had just enough room to create a communal spot where people could gather and sip a cocktail before dining or kick back and try our small-plates menu. It would be a cozy, low-lit, sexy setting. That little space became our lounge, an area of energetic cool that doesn't disrupt the dining scene. I love it when our neighbors pop in for our tropical Buena Vista rum punch and fried seppie or friends show up late at night and beg for Krispy Kreme "Coffee & Doughnuts."

These uncomplicated dishes feature quality ingredients with unexpected touches and can be easily re-created in your home. So dim the lights, put on some ambient tunes, and bring the Table 8 Lounge into your living room.

Isn't everybody a fan of the potato chip? Using a few drops of truffle oil, you can really enhance one of America's most beloved snacks. Quick, easy, delicious—but don't overdo it. You still want to taste the potato, so a few drops will go a long way. Use the truffle oil as an enhancer, not as a bulldozer.

Truffled Yukon Gold Potato Chips

SERVES: 8

DIFFICULTY: Easy

Vegetable oil, for frying	
Yukon Gold potatoes	2 medium, peeled
Sea salt and cracked black pepper to taste	
Truffle oil (white or black)	1 teaspoon

Heat the oil in a frying pan (no more than half full) or a fry basket to 350°F.

Using a mandoline, slice the potatoes super-thin so they are almost transparent. Working in batches, place the potato slices carefully in the oil, moving them around occasionally using metal tongs. They will cook quickly, so pull them out after about 3 minutes, when they are in the early stages of light golden brown and the bubbles in the oil begin to subside.

Line a large bowl with paper towels. Transfer the chips to the bowl and immediately season with the salt, pepper, and a very light drizzle of the truffle oil. Serve immediately. Leftovers will keep one day.

When you give love and attention to a pot of risotto to make *arancini*, the legendary street food of Sicily, it's like paying homage to each grain of rice. Meaning "little orange" in Italian (no doubt a play on the stuffed croquettes' size and saffron-tinged color), arancini are equally suitable for a midmorning pick-me-up or a late-night nibble. Here, a crispy golden coating of a double panko crust gives way to creamy mushroom risotto with a surprise of melted, oozing burrata cheese. You can save a step here by buying scallion oil at the grocer if it's available.

Wild Mushroom Risotto Balls /
Burrata / Scallion Oil

SERVES: 8

DIFFICULTY: Medium

SCALLION OIL

Scallions	2, thinly sliced
Grapeseed or canola oil	2 tablespoons

WILD MUSHROOM RISOTTO

Shiitake mushrooms	3, stems removed and sliced thin
Grapeseed or canola oil	1 tablespoon plus 1 teaspoon
Button mushrooms	3, stems removed and sliced thin
Chanterelle mushrooms	3, stems shaved and torn in shreds
Salt and cracked black pepper to taste	
Chicken stock or water	4 cups
Extra-virgin olive oil	2 tablespoons
Carnaroli rice	1 cup
Finely diced onion	2 tablespoons
Garlic	1 medium clove
Thyme	1 sprig
Bay leaf	1
White wine (preferably sauvignon blanc)	¼ cup
Unsalted butter	1 tablespoon
Finely grated Parmesan cheese	½ cup
Vegetable oil, for frying	
Burrata cheese	12 ounces, cut into ½-inch cubes
Panko Dustin' Mix (page 44)	2 cups
Egg	1, beaten with 1 tablespoon water
Salt	

ALTERN8: Substitute mozzarella, Monterey Jack, gouda, or any cheese that will melt as gooily as possible.

Basil and garlic oil will also work in lieu of scallion.

Place the scallions and 2 tablespoons grapeseed oil into a mortar and pestle. Coarsely grind the scallions until the oil has picked up the flavor and is emerald green in color. Allow it to steep in the oil, and reserve for garnish.

In a hot sauté pan over medium-high heat, sauté the mushrooms with 1 tablespoon plus 1 teaspoon of the grapeseed oil. Be careful not to move them around; you want to get a little color on one side. Season with salt and pepper, then flip and gently sauté the other side. This should take approximately 3 minutes. Remove from the heat and allow the mushrooms to cool. Coarsely chop them and set aside.

To prepare the risotto, bring the stock to a boil in a small sauce pot and set aside. In a medium, heavy-bottomed stockpot over medium-high heat, add the olive oil and the Carnaroli rice. Begin to stir the rice with a wooden spoon, coating and heating it in the oil—but not forming any color. Once the rice is completely warm to the touch but not toasted or colored, add the onion, garlic clove, thyme, and bay leaf, stirring constantly. Cook the vegetables until translucent, stirring all the while, about 5 minutes. Deglaze the pan with the white wine and reduce for 45 seconds, or until dry. Begin adding the stock, ¼ cup at a time while stirring, and add the next ¼ cup only after the preceding has been fully absorbed. After 10 minutes, reduce the heat to medium; after an additional 10 minutes, add a pinch of salt. Continue to cook and add the stock until the rice is perfectly al dente, or about

recipe continues...

25 minutes total cooking time. Remove from the heat, stir in the butter and Parmesan cheese, and season again with salt and pepper. Stir very well until incorporated. Add the chopped mushrooms, then spread the mixture onto a rimmed baking sheet lined with parchment paper. Smooth it out with a spatula, and refrigerate until cool.

While the risotto is cooling, heat 2 inches of frying oil in a small sauce pot until it reaches 350°F.

Get a bowl of water ready for your hands, because this will get messy. Moisten your hands and, like a sushi god, make 2-tablespoon portions of all the risotto and set aside. Place a portion of the rice in the palm of your hand, and flatten it into a fairly thin circle. Tuck a cheese cube firmly inside, squeeze it in, and then wrap around to make a nice rounded ball. You will need to continually wash your hands in order to prepare all the risotto balls.

Dip each wild mushroom risotto ball into the panko mix, then the egg wash, and back into the panko again. Fry in batches for approximately 2½ minutes, or until the bubbles begin to subside and the balls are nice and golden. Remove the risotto balls from the oil, season with salt, and drain on paper towels, allowing them to rest for 1 minute. Serve hot with a drizzle of scallion oil.

We often alter our menus according to what we're jonesing for, and when I pulled this together, I'd been craving a *fritto misto di mare*. Something about that coastal Italian dish—a lighter-than-air crispy mix of seafood and vegetables—spoke to me. I had squid's favorite partner, sepia, on hand in addition to some gorgeous baby artichokes, so I went for the *fritto simplo*. I shaved the chokes, bathed the cleaned seppie in the buttermilk and seasoned panko, and threw both ingredients in the fryer.

Fried Seppie / Fried Artichoke

SERVES: 8

DIFFICULTY: Medium

Vegetable oil, for frying	
Baby artichokes	8
Seppie	8 pieces, cleaned
Buttermilk	1 cup
Panko Dustin' Mix (page 44)	1 cup
Sea salt and cracked black pepper to taste	
Flat-leaf parsley	½ bunch
Lemon wedge, for garnish	

ALTERN8: Serve with aïoli (see pages 23 and 25).

Make a true fritto misto di mare with fried smelt, shrimp, eggplant, and, of course, a wedge of lemon.

You can purchase frozen seppie that's already cleaned if you don't want to deal with the procedure.

Heat the oil in a frying pan (no more than half full) or a fryer to 350°F.

Cut the top third off of each artichoke. Remove the outer leaves and the stem and discard. You will be left with the greenish-yellow inner core. With great care, slice thin on a mandoline.

Cut each sepia into ¼-inch strips, and dip into the buttermilk, and then into the panko mix. Be certain to really pack on the panko until the strips are thoroughly coated.

Line a large bowl with paper towels. Place the sliced artichokes into the hot oil and fry up until crisp, approximately 30 seconds to 1 minute. Remove from the pan into the bowl. Then fry the seppie until golden, also for 30 seconds to 1 minute. Remember to then turn off the heat under the oil. Add the seppie to the bowl of artichokes and immediately season with salt and pepper.

Once the oil has cooled down a bit, at the last moment (and being very careful of popping oil), toss the parsley leaves into the oil and let them fry for about 1 minute, until the bubbles stop. Add the fried parsley to the bowl, and serve immediately with the lemon.

Educ8: Sepia—Squid Pro Quo?

Deep-frying is a foolproof way to introduce the squeamish to seppie. When these creatures of the sea crisp up, you get slightly crunchy outer "shells" and tender, firm flesh beneath. Because these torpedo-shaped gems are the right size for a lounge bite, seppie can be stuffed and then grilled or fried.

Sepia, or cuttlefish as it's otherwise known, is a mollusk (not a fish) closely related to the squid. A bit larger and more tender than their cephalopod cousin, seppie are revered for their precious inky sacs. Though the pigment is best known for its use by artists since Roman times as an ink and dye, it's also important to Mediterranean cooking traditions. In and around Barcelona, you'll find the Catalans using the black-brown "juice" to flavor albóndigas con sepia, a meatball stew with peas and chunks of sepia, or the classic black rice arroz negre. In Venice, the delicacy is added to starchy risotto, while Sicilians use it to color wide noodles and toss them in an inky, garlic-infused sauce.

When you prepare cuttlefish, remember that cleaning is the key. First, snip the two long tentacles and then flip back the eight short "arms." Remove the eyes. As you squeeze from the middle center, the "beak" (or cuttlebone that helps the mollusk with buoyancy) will pop out. Discard that, and with the water running (trust me, your water bill might be a bit high from this), rinse the ink from the sepia until the water runs clear. Or, feel free to save the ink sac for later and add it to a stew or pasta, risotto, or paella.

How many times have you been to the supermarket and passed by a barrel filled with dried crystallized fish looking like shoe soles? You probably know it's good old salt cod, but the question remains: What to do with it?

In France, Spain, the Atlantic—basically anywhere that delicious cod is caught—lonely fishermen have survived by eating salt-cured cod. In modern days, when Gore-Tex and refrigerators allow for creature comfort on fishing boats, salt cod has outlived its necessity and found its way into a variety of culinary repertoires around Europe and North America.

Deep in the south of France along the Mediterranean coast, Provençal *brandade de morue* is an epic purée using reconstituted salt cod and a creamy blend of garlic, olive oil, and milk or cream. Mix in some boiled Yukon Gold potatoes to bind, and a little brandade makes for a rich, hearty side.

Once it has stiffened up for a day or so, I take the brandade and make baby fritters. Frying them in trusty panko dustin' mix produces a crusty exterior and flaky center—a perfect bar snack to accompany an ice-cold beer or a glass of chablis or sauvignon blanc. Don't forget that you'll also need twenty-four hours before you start to rid the cod of excess salt.

Brandade Fritters /
Wood-Roasted Tomato Coulis

MAKES:	Approximately 48 fritters
SERVES:	8 to 12
DIFFICULTY:	Medium

BRANDADE FRITTERS

Salt cod	1 pound, coarsely chopped
Yukon Gold potatoes	2 pounds, peeled and cubed
Heavy cream	1 cup
Extra-virgin olive oil	¼ cup
Chopped flat-leaf parsley	½ cup
Garlic	10 medium cloves, chopped
Canola oil for frying	
All-purpose flour	1 cup
Egg	1, beaten with 1 tablespoon water
Panko Dustin' Mix (page 44)	1 cup

WOOD-ROASTED TOMATO COULIS

Oregano	1 bunch
Thyme	½ bunch
Basil	½ bunch
Flat-leaf parsley	½ bunch
Ripe tomatoes	6, cores removed
Head of garlic, split apart	
Extra-virgin olive oil	3 tablespoons
Salt and pepper to taste	

ALTERN8: Garnish with fried parsley (see page 228).

For the salt cod, to get rid of excess salt, soak the cod for at least 24 hours and make sure to change the water a few times. Rinse well just before using.

To prepare the wood-roasted tomato coulis, prepare a gas or charcoal grill. Soak the herbs in water for 20 minutes.

In a large bowl, toss the tomatoes and garlic with 1 tablespoon of the olive oil. Place the herbs on the grill, forming a circular bed. Lay the tomatoes and garlic in a pyramid on top of them. Invert a large heat-proof bowl on top of the vegetables to seal in the heat. Check on the vegetables periodically as they cook, and remove any that become fully cooked. You are looking for the tomatoes to be roasted and just slightly charred, and the garlic should be just softening; the whole process should take about 30 minutes.

Once the vegetables are ready, remove and discard the charred herbs from the grill. Squeeze

recipe continues...

the garlic cloves out of their skins into a sauce pot and add the tomatoes and the remaining 2 tablespoons of olive oil. Simmer together for 15 minutes. Pass through a food mill or food processor, season with salt and pepper, and place in an ice-water bath to cool. The sauce should be the consistency of spaghetti sauce. If it's too runny at this point, place it in a stainless-steel sauce pot and slowly reduce over low heat to the correct consistency.

Place the salt cod and the potatoes in a large sauce pot. Bring to a boil in water (no need to add salt), and cook until very tender, approximately 15 minutes. Drain the water and place back over a medium flame to steam off excess moisture. Add the cream and simmer for about 10 minutes, stirring occasionally, to thicken the mixture, or until the cream reduces by half.

While the mixture simmers, place the olive oil in a small sauté pan over medium-high heat. Add the parsley and toast gently for about 30 seconds. Remove from the heat and add the parsley to the cod mixture, then add the garlic.

Run the mixture through a food mill (or a potato ricer), spread the brandade onto a baking pan, and allow to cool. If you prefer, you may prepare this the day before and really allow it to harden and stiffen. At this point, the mixture is ready to eat if you prefer not to fry it.

Or, to serve, heat the canola oil in a frying pan (no more than half full) or a fry basket to 350°F.

Form the cooled brandade into ¾-ounce fritters (about the size of a gumball). In three separate bowls, dip all the fritters into the flour, then into the egg wash, and finally give them a good roll in the panko mix. Allow them to set up in the freezer for a few minutes.

Line a large bowl with paper towels.

Working in batches, gently place the brandade fritters in the hot oil. These should fry up until just golden and warmed through, approximately 1 to 1½ minutes. Transfer the fritters to the bowl and immediately season very lightly with salt and pepper. Serve with the wood-roasted tomato coulis on the side, underneath, or drizzled on top.

The Scotch egg is a cheap and easy gastropub staple of the United Kingdom for late nights and early breakfasts. Back in the day at City Restaurant, we served these sausage-wrapped hard-boiled eggs at brunch. I was always fascinated by the meal-in-a-bite—and especially one that was deep-fried!

Instead of using beautiful giant hen eggs that we can purchase quite easily, for our lounge menu we decided to go with the smaller, more bite-size quail egg (ironically, this smaller egg commands awfully expensive prices). No sauce or garnish needed here, just breakfast in a ball!

Scotch Quail Eggs / Chorizo

MAKES: 8 eggs

DIFFICULTY: Easy

Quail eggs	8
Salt	
Canola oil, for frying	
Chorizo (page 41)	
All-purpose flour	1 cup
Egg	1, beaten with 1 tablespoon water
Panko Dustin' Mix (page 44)	1 cup
Pepper to taste	
Chervil, for garnish	

ALTERN8: Substitute the Spicy Lamb Sausage (page 69) for the chorizo.

Hard-boil the quail eggs for 5 minutes in salted water, then shock them quickly in an ice-water bath. Peel and place on a plate lined with a paper towel, then pat dry with another paper towel on top, being very careful because they are quite fragile.

Heat a small sauce pot with approximately 1 inch of canola oil to 350°F.

Pound a fist-size amount of the crumbles of uncooked chorizo into the palm of your hand using the same technique as with the risotto balls (see page 227). Place the egg inside, and carefully wrap the sausage around. Squeeze gently so that the sausage is tight around the egg and there is no air inside. Repeat with the remaining quail eggs.

Roll each of the eggs in the flour and then in the egg wash, then give it a nice pack in the panko mix. Fry for 3 minutes in the oil, or until golden. Drain on paper towels, season lightly with salt and pepper, garnish with the chervil, and serve.

What to do with a leftover baked potato?

For this recipe, leftovers actually work best, and you can serve the smashed spuds either hot or cold. Like a twice-baked potato, each spud here is first baked, then pan-fried. If you don't happen to have next-day bakers on hand but have a craving for something filling, pull out some small roasting potatoes and boil them, or salt-roast them (see page 238).

Use what you've got available to you: Pick your blue cheese according to preference, such as Roaring Forties for something a little spicier, or maybe something sweet and creamy like a Gorgonzola dolce. At the restaurant we use Kobe-style beef, but feel free to use your favorite cut.

Smashed Spuds / Sliced Beef / Blue Cheese

SERVES: 8	
DIFFICULTY: Easy	

Kosher salt	2 pounds
Small roasting potatoes	8, scrubbed and patted dry
Or leftover large potato	1, sliced into 8 pieces
Extra-virgin olive oil	2 tablespoons
New York strip steak	8 ounces
Salt and pepper to taste	
Blue cheese	2 ounces

If you don't have any leftover baked potatoes, preheat the oven to 400°F.

Pour the salt onto a rimmed baking sheet. Place the roasting potatoes in a small bowl and toss with 1 teaspoon of the oil. Place in a single layer on top of the kosher salt. (You can add woody herbs such as thyme, sage, or rosemary on the salt if you like for extra aromatics.) Cover with foil and roast the potatoes for approximately 25 minutes, or until cooked and fork tender. Remove the foil and allow the potatoes to cool. You can save the salt and re-use. Depending on their size, cut the potatoes in halves or quarters.

Season the steak with salt and pepper and heat a cast-iron pan over medium-high heat. Add 1 teaspoon of the oil and immediately place the steak in the pan. For medium rare, cook for about 2½ minutes on each side, then allow the steak to rest on a cutting board. Discard the oil from the pan and wipe away any remaining particles with a paper towel. Return the pan to the heat, and add the remaining oil. Place the

recipe continues...

Educ8: Salt-Roasting

With a naked baking sheet, you inevitably get burn marks on the bottom of your potatoes. Salt-roasting potatoes in a nest of rock or kosher salt is a great alternative. The salt the vegetables rest on conducts the heat more evenly than a flat surface would. Once the herbs are tossed in, they will infuse and penetrate for optimum flavor. Here, we use potatoes, but you can use this method to roast garlic (see page 120), or even baby beets.

So that there's no need to purchase enough rock salt to sprinkle your driveway after a snowstorm, you can re-use the salt. But when you do coat the potatoes, make sure that they're not dripping with oil. Too much oil causes the salt to coagulate and burn, imparting a bitter flavor that will prevent you from recycling the salt.

recipe continued...

potatoes skin side down on a sturdy surface and gently smash them, using a mallet. Season with salt and pepper.

Sauté the potatoes (either the roasted ones or the leftover large one) in the cast-iron pan until crisp on all sides. Remove to a plate lined with paper towels.

Slice the beef thin on a diagonal, and place on top of the smashed spuds on each of 8 plates or on a platter. Add a dollop of the blue cheese on top.

Along with the Seared Kobe Beef on Mini Yorkshire Pudding (page 67) and the Truffled Gruyère Fondue (page 201), this item has never left the lounge menu. I remember briefly intimating to a customer that I might be replacing the grilled cheese, and I was practically accosted! Because this snack is only available in the lounge and at the dining bar, people will go to sneaky lengths to order it. There have been guests who have left the table, walked to the lounge, ordered a sandwich, eaten it—and then returned to the table as if nothing had happened!

Like a cheesesteak to a Philadelphian, grilled cheese and short rib sandwiches are my comfort food for late-night lounging. And I can't get enough of the slow-cooked short rib. There are myriad uses for it, from picking and shredding it into a hash with roasted potatoes, garlic, and herbs to a hearty breakfast with poached or fried eggs and toast. Slice it and serve it with mashed potatoes. It may be a little time-consuming to braise anything (see page 161), especially without a slow cooker, but it's a dish that everyone should try at least once.

Grilled Cheese / Pulled Short Ribs
/ Pickled Red Onions

SERVES: 8

DIFFICULTY: Challenging

PULLED SHORT RIBS

Grapeseed or canola oil	1 tablespoon
Boneless beef short ribs	2 pounds
Salt and pepper to taste	
Carrot	½, cut into large dice
Celery	½, cut into large dice
Onion	½, cut into large dice
Garlic	6 medium cloves, cracked
Red wine (such as cabernet sauvignon)	1 cup
Sachet (page 47)	
Beef broth	3 cups
Sourdough bread	2-pound loaf, cut into 16 slices
Bel Paese cheese	12 ounces, sliced thin
Pickled Red Onions (page 35)	2 tablespoons plus 2 teaspoons
Unsalted butter	4 teaspoons, room temperature
Grapeseed oil	4 teaspoons

ALTERN8: If you have a slow cooker, you can make the short ribs ahead of time.

Any good-quality melting cheese, such as Wisconsin Cheddar, will work well.

We make a "true" grilled cheese and grill the sandwich on our wood-burning grill. You should try that at home!

Preheat the oven to 325°F.

Beginning with a large saucepan or braising pan with a lid, heat the tablespoon of grapeseed oil over medium-high heat. Season the short ribs with salt and pepper. Sear the short ribs on either side until caramelized and golden brown, about 5 minutes. Remove the meat from the pan. Add the carrot and celery to the pan and cook for 5 minutes over the same heat. Add the onion and garlic. Cook together until caramelized, about 5 minutes, stirring occasionally as needed. Add the short ribs back to the pan and deglaze with the red wine. Add the sachet and, stirring from time to time, allow the wine to reduce until almost evaporated, about 6 minutes. Pour in the beef broth and bring the braise up to a boil. Put the lid on and place in the oven for 2 hours. Stir occasionally.

After the first 2 hours of cooking time, remove the lid. For the next hour, baste the short ribs every 15 minutes, leaving the lid off. Cook for an additional hour, until very tender, for a total of 4 hours cooking time.

recipe continues...

recipe continued...

Pull the short ribs from the oven and allow them to cool in the braising juices for at least a few hours. Carefully transfer the meat to a plate and strain the juices through a fine sieve, then allow the fat to rise. Remove the fat. Using a dinner fork in each hand, lightly shred the meat along the natural grains in a pulling motion from the center outward, and set aside.

To prepare each sandwich, begin by preheating the oven to 350°F.

Take 2 slices of bread. On the bottom slice, place a layer of cheese (you'll want approximately 1½ ounces for each sandwich, just enough to cover the bread to the edges), then top with 1 teaspoon of pickled red onion, spread to the sides. Place ¼ cup of the pulled short ribs on top, add another layer of cheese, and top with the second slice of bread. Brush each completed sandwich on top and bottom with ½ teaspoon butter.

In a cast-iron pan over medium-high heat, add 1 teaspoon of the grapeseed oil and allow it to get nice and hot. Place 2 sandwiches in at a time and flip so they will absorb the oil on both sides. Weight them down with a small sauté pan. After 1 minute, flip the sandwiches, return the weight, and place directly in the oven. After 2 minutes, remove the weight. Flip the sandwich one final time, and cook for 1 final minute. Pull from the oven, slice diagonally, and serve immediately. Repeat with the remaining sandwiches.

After our first anniversary at Table 8, I was dying to serve a rustic grilled pizza. Using the dough recipe on page 45, I experimented with some simple accompaniments and arrived at this dish.

These pizzettas, fired up on a wood-burning grill, were an instant hit. Running into space issues with the grill, it was pretty challenging—even for Javier, my line cook of ten years—to have eight pizzettas cooking alongside five Kobe flatirons, four baby chickens, and the usual handful of grilled cheese with pulled short ribs . . . but what a good run it was!

Grilled Pizzetta /
Roasted Artichoke / Tomato / Red Hawk Cheese

SERVES: 8

DIFFICULTY: Easy

Baby artichokes	8
Unsalted butter	1 tablespoon
Extra-virgin olive oil	1 tablespoon, plus more for brushing
Thyme	1 sprig
Garlic	2 small cloves
Salt and pepper to taste	
Pizzetta Dough (page 45)	8 2-ounce portions (the size of a Ping-Pong ball)
Red Hawk cheese	½ pound, thinly sliced
Roasted Tomatoes (page 39)	1 batch
Julienne of basil, for garnish	

ALTERN8: Substitute Camembert or Taleggio if you are not able to find Red Hawk online or at the local gourmet food store.

TOP THESE PIZZETTAS INSTEAD WITH:
Chorizo (page 41), Salsa Verde (page 29), shaved Manchego cheese

Cracked Green Olives (page 33), Warm Anchovy Vinaigrette (page 187), torn basil

Smoked Sturgeon (page 175), Onion Soubise (page 145)

To pan-roast the artichokes, begin by cutting the top third off of each artichoke. Remove the outer leaves and the stem, and discard. You will be left with the greenish-yellow inner core. Split in half lengthwise. Place a cast-iron pan over medium-low heat. Add the butter and olive oil. Once the butter is melted, add the thyme and garlic cloves. Add the artichokes and, without jostling the pan, roast for about 4 minutes, or until caramelized and cooked through. Turn off the heat, flip the artichokes, and allow them to stay in the pan and finish cooking for a few minutes until fork tender. Season with salt and pepper.

Preheat the oven to 475°F.

If you don't have a pizza stone, brush a large cast-iron pan lightly with olive oil. Once the pizzetta dough is completely thawed, stretch and shape each portion into a ⅛-inch-thick disk. Season the dough with salt and pepper and place the first disk in the cast-iron pan. Allow it to cook over medium-high heat, flipping

recipe continues...

once so it's evenly cooked, until it's nice and golden, about 6 minutes. Repeat with the remaining dough disks.

Add the Red Hawk cheese, about 1 ounce for each pizzetta. Add 4 slices of roasted artichoke and 3 pieces of roasted tomato atop each pizzetta. Place directly in the oven and bake until the cheese just bubbles, about 4 minutes. Slice evenly, top with the basil, and serve.

(On a grill, follow the same preparation for the dough. Heat up the grill, stretch the dough, season it, then place it over the lightly greased grill until golden, about 3 minutes. Add the toppings and finish it in the oven for 4 minutes at 400°F.)

When creating the menu for RokBar in Hollywood, I was in my office just racking my brain trying to come up with a comforting, slightly junky down-home dessert. I was snacking on a Krispy Kreme doughnut and drinking my morning coffee, and then came the coffee-doughnut connection. What about a doughnut bread pudding with a dollop of espresso whipped cream on top? I couldn't wait to make it, and for ultimate decadence, this nails it.

Krispy Kreme "Coffee & Doughnuts"

SERVES: 8

DIFFICULTY: Easy

Krispy Kreme "original glazed" doughnuts	18, each sliced in 6 pieces
Heavy cream	1 quart
Whole milk	2 cups
Egg yolks	10
Eggs	2
Sweetened condensed milk	½ cup
Butter, for greasing the baking dish	
Brewed espresso, cooled	½ cup

Preheat the oven to 250°F.

Line 2 baking sheets with parchment paper. Spread the doughnut pieces on the baking sheets and bake for about 30 minutes, or until dry on the outside and semi-firm in the center. Set aside.

In a large bowl, whisk 2 cups of the cream with the milk, egg yolks, whole eggs, and condensed milk. Add the doughnut pieces and let them soak until they are softened, about 1 hour. Stir every 15 minutes.

Raise the oven temperature to 350°F.

Lightly butter a 9 x 13-inch baking dish. Spoon the doughnut mixture into the dish and cover with aluminum foil. Set the dish in a roasting pan large enough to hold it, and add approximately ½ inch of water to the pan. Bake the pudding in the water bath for 40 minutes. Remove the foil and bake the pudding for an additional 20 minutes, or until the custard is set. Try the old test of dipping a paring knife into the center of the pudding to see if the custard has completely set.

Preheat the broiler. Being quite vigilant, broil the pudding for 3 minutes, or until the top is lightly browned. Allow the pudding to cool for about 30 minutes.

In a medium bowl, whip the remaining 2 cups of cream into semi-soft peaks. Stir in the espresso, and serve alongside the doughnut bread pudding.

Kona Coffee Kicker

SERVES: 1

DIFFICULTY: Easy

Coffee liqueur	¾ ounce
Brandy	½ ounce
Stoli Vanil vodka	½ ounce
Hot Kona Gold coffee	
Freshly whipped cream, to garnish	
Small pinch of fresh coffee grounds	

Pour the liqueur, brandy, and vodka into an Irish coffee glass. Add the fresh hot coffee to within an inch of the rim. Spoon ¾ inch of whipped cream on top, and garnish with the coffee grounds. Serve immediately.

After you've enjoyed the decadent Krispy Kreme "Coffee & Doughnuts" (page 247), here's your next logical step. I typically don't serve coffee drinks, since winters in Los Angeles are so mild, but this hot little toddy features the prized star of javaworld: Kona coffee. The 100-percent pure estate Kona from Aloha Island Coffee Company that we serve at Table 8 is like gold—and because it's low in acid and naturally sweet with faint notes of chocolate, it's happily married with a little vodka and liqueur. A highly efficient caffeine delivery system, this "Kicker" is a great way to end a meal and start the next phase of the late-night revelry (shenanigans and all).

If I can't be sitting on the beach, climbing a coconut palm, or deep-sea fishing in Barbados, this cocktail takes me there. I made this drink with Tito, a bartender who has been with Table 8 since we opened. The combination of two types of rum goes surprisingly well with a splash of peach schnapps.

Buena Vista Rum Punch

SERVES: 1

DIFFICULTY: Easy

Crushed ice	
Mount Gay vanilla-flavored Barbados rum	2 ounces
Captain Morgan's spiced rum	½ ounce
Juice of ½ lime	
Splash of peach schnapps	

Fill a rocks glass one third of the way with crushed ice. Load up the cocktail shaker with ice, and pour in the two rums, the lime juice, and the schnapps. Shake vigorously and pour over the crushed ice. Serve immediately.

Until recently, guaro wasn't available in the United States, but little by little, it's popping up on shelves as the hot new import. Widely considered the "official" national drink of Costa Rica, this smooth grain alcohol is consumed by the boatload with an anthology's worth of drinking songs. Guaro is traditionally served with Coca-Cola or soda water and lots of limes (known as a Costa Libre as opposed to a rum-based Cuba Libre). Native to this tropical land of rain forests, sandy beaches, and brooding volcanoes, guaro also mixes well with exotic fruits. My uncle Marvin in Costa Rica instructs that you must stir any guaro cocktail with your finger ten times clockwise and ten times counter-clockwise and then taste it right off the finger. Maybe for good luck? Never really asked . . . I just did it.

Needless to say, this "juice" really packs a punch; the sliced fruit macerates overnight in the alcohol and absorbs a lot of it, which mellows the grain spirit. Consuming all that drunken fruit might cause an evening of hanging out with friends and family to get a little goofy.

Guaro Goofy Juice

SERVES: 8

DIFFICULTY: Easy

Apples	2 large, cut into bite-size pieces
Oranges	3 medium, cut into segments
Strawberries	1 pint, cut into bite-size pieces
Brown sugar	½ cup
Guaro or grain alcohol like Everclear	1 bottle or 3¼ cups
Malibu rum	½ bottle (375 ml)
Orange juice	1 quart
Mango purée	½ cup
7-Up	1 liter

Place the apples, oranges, and strawberries into a large bowl. Toss with the brown sugar and add the guaro. Allow this mixture to soak overnight in the refrigerator.

In a large punch bowl, mix the rum, orange juice, and mango purée. Add the drunken fruit and any leftover liquid, then top off with the 7-Up. Serve in chilled glasses.

sources

Specialty Gourmet and Ethnic Foods

Bangkok Market
4757 Melrose Avenue
Los Angeles, CA 90029
323-662-9705

Bristol Farms
www.bristolfarms.com

Browne Trading Company
Merrill's Wharf
Portland, ME 04101
800-944-7848
www.browne-trading.com

Dean & DeLuca
www.deandeluca.com

Ferry Building Marketplace
One Ferry Building
San Francisco, CA 94111
415-693-0996
www.ferrybuildingmarketplace.com

Marshall Field's
www.fields.com

Surfas
8777 W. Washington Boulevard
Culver City, CA 90232
866-799-4770
www.surfasonline.com

Sur La Table
www.surlatable.com

Whole Foods Market
www.wholefoodsmarket.com

Zingerman's
www.zingermans.com

Cheese

Cowgirl Creamery
80 Fourth Street
Point Reyes Station, CA 94956
415-663-9335
www.cowgirlcreamery.com

Gioia Cheese Co.
1605 Potrero Avenue
South El Monte, CA 91733
626-444-6015
gioiacheese@hotmail.com

Jasper Hill Farm
P.O. Box 272
Greensboro, VT 05841
www.jasperhillfarm.com

Murray's Cheese
254 Bleecker Street
New York, NY 10014
888-MY-CHEEZ (692-4339)
www.murrayscheese.com

Sally Jackson Cheeses
16 Nealy Road
Oroville, WA 98844
509-485-3722
www.sallyjacksoncheeses.com

Uplands Cheese Company
4540 County Road ZZ
Dodgeville, WI 53533
888-935-5558
www.uplandscheese.com

Valley Shepherd Creamery
50 Fairmount Road
Long Valley, NJ 07853
908-876-3200
www.valleyshepherdcreamery.com

Wisconsin Cheese
www.wisdairy.com

Meat and Seafood

Bristol Farms
www.bristolfarms.com

Browne Trading Company
Merrill's Wharf
Portland, ME 04101
800-944-7848
www.browne-trading.com

Hoffman Game Birds
Manteca, CA 95337
209-823-4028

Manchester Farms
P.O. Box 97
Dalzell, SC 29040
800-845-0421
www.manchesterfarms.com

New Zealand Lamb
www.nzbeeflamb.co.nz

Niman Ranch
www.nimanranch.com

Prairie Harvest
P.O. Box 1013
Spearfish, SD 57783
800-350-7166
www.prairieharvest.com

Snake River Farms
1555 Shoreline Drive, 3rd Floor
Boise, ID 83702
www.snakeriverfarms.com

Sonoma County Poultry
P.O. Box 140
Penngrove, CA 94951
707-795-3797
www.libertyducks.com

Produce and Farmers

Coastal Organics
Maryann and Paul Carpenter
Santa Paula, CA 93060
805-983-3064

Coleman Family Farms
Bill Coleman
Carpinteria, CA 93013
805-684-5569

Ferry Plaza Farmers Market
Tuesday, Thursday, Saturday, Sunday
One Ferry Building
San Francisco, CA 94111
415-693-0996
http://www.ferryplazafarmersmarket.com/markets/

Melissa's
P.O. Box 21127
Los Angeles, CA 90021
800-588-0151
www.melissas.com

Philip McGrath Farms
505 North Wood Road
Camarillo, CA 93010
805-485-4210
mcgrath.familyfarms@verizon.net

Santa Monica Farmer's Market
Wednesdays, 8:30 a.m. – 1:30 p.m.
Arizona Avenue and Second Street
Santa Monica, CA 90401
http://santa-monica.org/farmers_market

Shaner Farms
Peter Shaner
Valley Center, CA 92082
760-749-9376

Windrose Farm
5750 El Pharo Road
Paso Robles, CA 93446
805-239-3757
www.windrosefarm.org

Wine

Arrowood Vineyards
14347 Sonoma Highway
Glen Ellen, CA 95442
800-938-5170
www.arrowoodvineyards.com

Ferrari-Carano
8761 Dry Creek Road
Healdsburg, CA 95448
707-433-6700
www.ferrari-carano.com

Newton Vineyard
2555 Madrona Avenue
St. Helena, CA 94574
707-963-9000
www.newtonvineyard.com

Roederer Estate
4501 Highway 128
Philo, CA 95466
707-895-2288
www.roedererestate.net

Seghesio Family Vineyards
14730 Grove Street
Healdsburg, CA 95448
707-433-3579
www.seghesio.com

Siduri Winery
980 Airway Court, Suite C
Santa Rosa, CA 95403
707-578-3882
www.siduri.com

Stuhlmuller Vineyards
4951 West Soda Rock Lane
Healdsburg, CA 95448
707-431-7745
www.stuhlmullervineyards.com

index